Basic Guide to the Rottweiler

*Written by breeders
who know the breed...
For those who are interested in
learning more about the
Rottweiler*

To all those who have challenged me: "Here's to you......."

Printed in the United States of America

ISBN 0-932045-08-1
Library of Congress Catalog Card Number 94-72579

Front Cover:
Falko vom Steinkopf, SchH III, AD, ZtP, TT, IPO III, WH, Korung
Owned by Frank & Laura Alfano, Alfalar Farms
Tampa, Fl — See Page 64

Back Cover:
V-1 USRC Select and 1994 Ontario Siegerin, Nighthawk's Abkussen
SchH I, B, Am/Can CD, HIC, TDI, TT, CGC, AKC and CKC pointed,
MRC Honor Roll, CRC Bronze Achievement, ARC Bronze Dam, OFA
Good and CERF
Breeder/Owner/Handler: Daviann Brooks, Nighthawk Rottweilers,
Beverly Hills, CA — See Page 64

The *Basic Guide to the Rottweiler* is written from information collected about the breed from some of the top breeders in the nation. In this way the material presented is not only breed specific, but is an overview of the breed as seen by many kennels and breeders, not the breed as viewed by a single individual and limited to their experiences. We would like to thank the following people for their help in putting this project together.

Michael R. Zervas - Managing Editor
Stephen W. Jones - Project Editor
Melissa Stirling - Project Coordinator

And a special thank you for the tremendous help we received from the following owners, breeders and of course, lovers of the Rottweiler.

CONTRIBUTING AUTHORITIES IN NO PARTICULAR ORDER:

Dr. Swift	Robert & Patricia Baker	Barry & Lori Fiandra
Mike & Ann Stroud	Colonial Rottweiler Club	Victoria Weaver
Linda Atzbach	Todd & Bridget Intravartolo	Henry & Ellen Walls
Monica Sellers	Karen & Harold Riddle Jr.	Maria Fox
Art Twiss	Dr. Royce & Marilyn Poel	Cubby Lash
Barbara J. Wrede	Norma Dikeman	Gwen Chaney
Tonya Renee Jones	John & Kristy Peixoto	Dr. E.A. Corley
Wayne Budwick	Stephen & Charlotte Johnson	Janna Morgan
Carol Wall	Drs. John & Margaret Zazzaro	James Spencer
Tony DiCicco	George & Betty Chamberlin	Bonnie Rosenburg
Adrienne Perry	Don & Elizabeth Kressley	Patricia Major
Karyn Day	Allen & Loretta Pyeatt	Joan Eversole, DMD
Matt & Lorene Jones	Ron & Anne K. Yatteau	Frank & Laura Alfano
Daviann Brooks	Tom & Laura Wurstner	Mike & Mary Donahue
Linda Gunderson	Don & Patricia Rennick	Bob Gregory
Alexis Cruser	Rich & Linda Berberich	Pamela Brown
Gladys Trout	Tom & Barbara McCuen	Merri Van Dyke
Rebecca Lantz	Comann & Marge Gold	Kris Dorko
Dr. Colin Hagan	Nicholas Dorko, Jr. DMV	Carolyn Ferguson
United Schutzhund Clubs of America		

Your years of knowledge and interest in the breed, has not only made this book possible, but it insures the future of the Rottweiler.

HOW TO USE THE
BASIC GUIDE BREED SERIES

This series of books is written for the person who is investigating the breed for a possible pet; for the person who has decided on a Rottweiler and wants to know how to find a good breeder and what to ask; for the person who has just bought a Rottweiler who wants to know what to expect and how to train it; and for the person who owns a Rottweiler who wants to know more about the breed and how closely his or her dog resembles current champions of the breed. These books are also a *beginning point* for those who want to know what else they can do with their dogs.

The Basic Guide to the Rottweiler takes a unique approach. Instead of being the opinion of one kennel, with one style of dog and one view of the breed, we have interviewed many breeders and have pooled their vast knowledge and interest in the breed to create an overview as **NO OTHER BREED BOOK** provides. The knowledge and experience reflected here are not limited to a single person.

This series is truly educational for the reader. In many places, where breeders have given us conflicting information, we have pooled that information, making note that there is dispute within the breed and indicating that further discussion with individual breeders is advisable.

OUR TWO SPECIAL SECTIONS

The **HALL OF FAME** section not only puts new people in contact with breeders of top quality animals as a place to start their search, but it also gives the reader a chance to see the different styles within the breed. By carefully studying the pedigrees provided, it is a start in understanding the relation of the pedigree to the individual dog - the cornerstone upon which breeds and breed registries are built. If you already own a Rottweiler, you might enjoy looking through this section and comparing your dog and its pedigree with those who have been achievers in the world of dogs!

Finally, the **SHOPPING ARCADE** section puts readers in contact with some of the fine businesses whose products relate to dogs and to Rottweilers in particular. For those of us who show dogs on a regular basis, we meet some of these fine specialty businesses every week. For those who do not attend such events, the Shopping Arcade section provides a chance to find these quality products which will make excellent gifts for the breed lover, additions to your home, or products to help you raise a happy, healthy dog.

BEFORE YOU BUY A DOG

1) Decide WHAT YOU WANT THE DOG TO DO. Evaluate your home and lifestyle and how a dog should fit into your life.

2) Look at different breeds and decide what breed is best for you and your home.

3) Realize that there are differences in style and temperament within each breed. Different breeders select their breeding stock based on different criteria. Use the Hall of Fame to help you see the differences among dogs and kennels.

4) Find a breeder who produces dogs which will fit your needs. Ask questions which will insure that the dog you buy will be right for you by finding a breeder who places importance on the qualities which are important to you.

5) Be sure to ask the breeder the right questions for that particular breed and be prepared for what the breeder will want to ask you.

With this in mind, your decision will be an informed one and the dog you buy will be a welcome addition to your family for years to come.

Table of Contents

Section I

Section II

This famous photo of a Rottweiler pup has been featured on calendars and T-shirts. It shows the personality of the breed, its easy going manner and the ease and power of movement which are evident even in a puppy.

INTRODUCTION

We are often asked, *"Why buy a purebred dog?"* Certainly there are some wonderful, loving and even talented mutts. But have you ever owned a dog, or known a mutt you admired and been frustrated in trying to locate another like him?

Centuries ago, people kept dogs for pets, for working partners in their fields and with their flocks, as hunting companions, and for protection of the family. As dogs began to diversify, people noticed certain dogs were better at one thing than others. People liked the looks of one dog over another, or found that one had better instincts in certain areas. Dogs in one geographic area began to look alike from interbreeding within a small population, and people who lived in other areas came to buy such dogs when they wanted a certain characteristic or look. Thus dog breeds began to evolve. The breeds were based on predictability of looks and performance in a dog from a certain area or gene pool.

Breeders, and later field or kennel clubs began to keep records of individuals. This recording of the gene pool is a second step in creating a breed. Without such record keeping, a breed will change and lose characteristics. Again, it is insurance that a puppy will grow to look and act like certain other individuals.

Finally, people wrote descriptions of the breed. At first these were simply descriptions of certain dogs which impressed the author on a hunt, or in traveling. These descriptions are our earliest written standards. Later, breeders banded together to form breed clubs and they wrote a detailed, collective description of the breed for others to follow. Careful breeders who studied the standard, thought about the original purpose of the breed, and were concerned about health and temperament, continued the breed.

The value of a breed, and a registration to record it, is that a buyer of a puppy can predict what it will look like when it is grown up, what its talents and temperament will be and how well it will fit a living situation. If we owned and raised nothing but crossbreeds, or if you simply got a cute puppy from the dog pound, you would have no way of knowing what type of dog might be sharing your home and your life for the next twelve to fourteen years!

And there is a certain pride of ownership in a stylish, quality dog. It does not take an experienced eye to tell the difference between a fine antique and a fake, between a fine luxury car and a clunker. To say that there is no reason to get a purebred dog instead of a mutt is like saying that a Geo will get you there just as well as a Cadillac. Both fill the same job of taking the driver from one place to another, but the pride of ownership is entirely different. It does not take training to recognize quality in an animal. It is manifested in the way the dog comes together, the way the over-all animal pleases the eye, the attitude and presence — self confidence — of the dog. Good breeding, soundness, and aptitude of purpose are a source of *pleasure. If you divide the cost of the average puppy from a good breeder, by the life span of the dog, you will be paying less than fifty dollars a year, or about four dollars a month for the pleasure of an animal that will be recognizable as his breed, serve the purpose for which he was bred, and have the health and temperament that will match your family and life-style.*

In this way, you will find an animal that will be a good fit, one that will share your home and your love for a lifetime, instead of getting a puppy that grows into an individual you cannot live with, and one which causes frustration and stress.

Breeders find that new owners who take this kind of time to locate a puppy are far more likely to be satisfied with their new family member. They are more likely to realize what care of that breed will entail, will be more likely to provide a good home, and far less likely to take it to the pound or otherwise get rid of the animal.

So, take the time to do your homework about the breed. A dog is not only what it looks like, but how easy it is to live with in a given situation. No breed is perfect for everyone. Find out what questions to ask for that particular breed, locate breeders, and take your time to find a puppy or adult dog which will meet your needs. For those purposes, we hope these BASIC GUIDE *books will be helpful.*

HISTORY

Many of the dog breeds covered in this series came from specific origins and were bred for a single purpose. This historic purpose is the "check" against which modern breeders measure the progress of their breed; i.e., they ask themselves if the individual dog they are breeding would be able to carry out its original function. Thus a sight hound which had to run would need good movement, and a guard dog would need a good bite.

This kind of checking is much more difficult for the Rottweiler, since it was not bred for a single purpose, but for a multitude of purposes. This is why there is such a wide variety of types and styles within the breed. The Rottweiler is a breed of many different functions, contradictions, styles and temperaments. When considering a Rottweiler it is of utmost importance to evaluate what you want in a dog and to take the time to find a dog from a reputable breeder which will suit your goals. To do anything less is to court disaster.

In dog breeding, dogs which were kept by royalty and wealthy families had a single purpose. Families of wealth and nobility throughout the world could afford to keep large kennels and selectively breed dogs for their own enjoyment. The man of the house had dogs for hunting, even dogs for different types of hunting. The women had companion dogs, often lap dogs, which kept them company while they led pampered and often sedentary lives. War dogs and guard dogs were used to protect the estates and support the legions of the wealthy. Herding dogs helped the estate workers manage livestock. These domestic helpers of mankind were selectively bred to be successful for those single purposes. Because of that singleness of purpose, traits within the breed were uniform, their consistency being in keeping with the job at hand.

But the Rottweiler was a poor man's dog. Working people did not have the money to keep breeding stock, nor to feed several dogs to do each of the many tasks required of a dog who lived and served a working family. One dog was expected to be a friend to the children, a working companion for the man of the house and a protector of the family. As the man's work changed throughout the year, so did the dog's. The only consistent traits a dog needed were a high degree of intelligence and a willingness to please his master. Devotion and the substance and agility to do a number of different tasks were the most sought-after traits and were consistently bred into the animals rather than the talent for a single, specific task.

The Rottweiler sprang from a rural area of Europe, an area of isolated valleys surrounded by high mountains, and inhabited by working people who lived in small towns and villages which hung along mountain ridges, and often along rivers and trade routes. Over the centuries, these people did a variety of tasks and their lives ebbed and flowed with the influences which washed over Europe. The lives of their dogs changed and conformed to the lives of their masters.

The Rottweiler is both a new breed, having evolved into its present form only within this century, and an ancient breed, bringing its traits forward from the times when Roman armies moved into Europe and what is now Germany, bringing with them their dogs. In between, the Rottweiler may have been what we would today recognize as several different breeds, or at least several different varieties within a breed. During the late 1800's and the early part of this century, the breed was recognized and represented by several different clubs, each with its own goals, standards and sometimes hostile attitudes toward the others.

From the early point in history when the Rottweiler began to evolve as a breed, he has been used for a number of different purposes. This multitude of purpose is one reason why there is a variety of style, temperament and size in the Rottweiler today.

This contributed to both the versatility and the variety within this breed. It has also made it difficult for present day breeders, in that they cannot look back at a single purpose and measure the ability of the present day stock to do the task for which it was bred. That is why, in our section on "Dog Shows and Other Competitions," you will notice the wide variety of tasks a Rottweiler can perform well. In our "Hall of Fame" section, you will see more titles, and a wider variety of titles, attached to the names of our featured dogs in this book than in any other book of this series.

The Rottweiler takes its name from the town and area of Rottweil in southern Germany. This town is located in a valley near the source of the Neckar River which is 371 kilometers long and borders the Black Forest. The river enters the Rhine at Mannheim, just above Heidelberg. This long valley also produced the Leonberger, a breed which is still found in Europe, though not recognized by the American Kennel Club (AKC). In ancient times, the Romans moved over the Alps and through this area on their way to establish the town of Trier in Germany. The Romans brought the food for their army on the hoof, and used their cattle dogs to bring along the herds behind the army.

By the Middle Ages, the area found itself at the crossroads of major trade routes and it became an important marketplace in Central Europe, trading grains, cattle and merchant's wares. The Town Hall in Rottweil is a Gothic structure dating back to 1521. Churches in the town date back as early as the 13th century.

The butcher became an important person in the area, for he provided meat for caravans of traders moving through the area. In those days, the butcher's job had a much wider scope than we think of today. He brought the cattle to market. For this task, he used his dog to help him herd the livestock. Once the cattle were ready for slaughter, a dog was used to bait the bulls before slaughter. It was believed that the meat from an animal which had been killed during or immediately after physical activity gave more tender meat than meat from animals slaughtered straight from the fields or holding areas. The event of bull baiting also called public attention to the fact that a slaughter would soon take place, and brought the customers to the butcher's door. After the slaughter, the dog was hooked to a draft cart and used to deliver the meat. This is where the term "The Butcher's Dog" came about, referring to the Rottweiler.

One of our breeders pointed out that old German studies of the breed also refer to the Rottweiler as the "Drover's Dog," indicating his use as a herding dog. But as a herding dog alone, the Rottweiler would have been much different. He would have had the temperament and physical appearance of a more typical dog in the herding group such as the German Shepherd or the Border Collie. The appearance of and psychological makeup of the Rottweiler is far different. He does not bark frequently, nor does he have the high activity of those breeds. He does not have the low, light build, nor the fluid agility of a dog specifically bred for tending flocks and herds. Instead he has the broad mouth and head piece, the substance and square stance of the mastiff types of dogs, bred for centuries as war dogs, fighting dogs, guard dogs and bull baiting breeds. Yet he also has the broad back, size, powerful muscles, heavy build and quiet temperament of carting breeds such as the Newfoundland, Saint Bernard, and Great Pyrenees. Merchants, bakers and craftsman of all kinds widely used the dog to carry goods and make deliveries along the narrow streets. It is possible that the draft dogs of 150 years ago were as large as those of today, but were lighter in build, or at least longer in leg, with more daylight under their bodies. Their skulls were less wide, with longer, more pointed muzzles.

Other families in the area with flocks of sheep, goats or fowl, tended to keep dogs which were small enough so that the lighter livestock was not endangered or overpowered by the dog. These dogs were more like dogs of the herding breeds. But if the family herded cattle, the broader mouthed, heavier dog was needed to keep the bulls in line and to shove a stubborn cow along its way. Thus, over the centuries, the Rottweiler was probably more like several breeds, all generically termed by the name of the region from which they sprang.

In the late 19th century, fate turned against the Rottweiler. Laws were passed which not only made bull baiting illegal, but also made it illegal to use a dog as a draft animal. Donkeys replaced dogs for draft work. Herding cattle was no longer done on foot over long distances, and cattle breeds changed, eliminating the need for a dog which had the size and tenacity to handle the coarse, ill-tempered bulls of the earlier centuries. In short, by the turn of the century, the Rottweiler found himself unemployed.

As the need for the dogs declined, so did their breeding. By 1905, only a single Rottweiler bitch lived within the town from which the breed had taken its name. But the same trade routes which had carried the goods and services of the area throughout Europe had also carried its dogs throughout middle Europe.

The first attempt to describe the breed did not come until 1883, when the first breed standard was written. The breed standard is a description, or an attempt to codify the characteristics of a breed, laying down a blueprint for later breeders. It is by this standard,

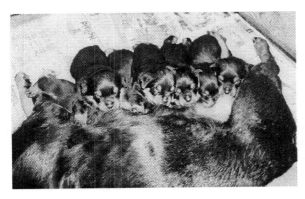

or blueprint of the breed, that breeders select their breeding stock and perpetuate those characteristics which set one breed apart from another. This first breed standard for the Rottweiler was not published or widely circulated until some eighteen years later, in 1901.

With the turn of the century came an international interest in dogs, dog breeds, and the need for breed clubs to preserve each breed. Many of the modern breed clubs were formed around that time. Originally a Loenberger and Rottweiler Breed Club was formed, but it split in 1907, and two clubs appeared which were dedicated exclusively to the Rottweiler. One of these clubs, formed in Heidelberg, Germany, in turn split over political differences between factions. The splinter group did not last long and was absorbed into a third club, the International Rottweiler Club. This club wrote a new standard, which differed somewhat from that of any of the previous clubs.

Then an interesting event took place in Germany. The Rottweiler was officially recognized as a fourth police dog breed, following the German Shepherd Dog, the Doberman and the Airedale Terrier. This gave the Rottweiler yet another "job," one which has continued to this day, and it placed emphasis on developing the aspects of the dog's personality which were useful in that line of work. This more aggressive characteristic was not a widely developed aspect of the breed temperament up to that time.

In 1921, after more than a year of intense negotiation, the two remaining clubs merged to form the General German Rottweiler Club (ADRK). Since that time there has only been one German club representing the breed. It set out to unify the breed under one controlling body, to eliminate the variations in type which existed under the previous diverse clubs, and to create a single standard. A decision was made in 1923 to eliminate all colors except black and tan, and to register and recognize only dogs whose parents were registered in the breed book. There was a long-coated variety which was also eliminated at that time, though, as with many other breeds which have dropped a long coated variety, that coat will occasionally still pop up today.

The large, powerful build and strong head are characteristic of the breed.

Because the ADRK believes the breed should be a working dog, not simply a dog of impressive appearance, they introduced strict limitations on breeding stock, taking into account working ability and temperament. Some of the titles you will see in the Hall of Fame are from this German registry. Under these guidelines, levels of working competence must be met before a dog or bitch can be bred.

By 1926, when the Allgemeiner Deutscher Rottweiler Klub (ADRK) published *The Rottweiler in Word and Picture*, there were two sizes of Rottweiler. The author cited two types: the larger dog used for draft work, and the smaller, herding type. Although there is no mention of size or weight, the work goes on to describe the differences between the two types, and states that they were not interbred. The differences between the two sizes included, as might be expected, a difference in temperament; the larger dogs being quieter. Color is also interesting. The draft dogs, like many draft horse breeds, established a rich color which was maintained. Uniformity of color and pleasing structure, or conformation, has long been associated with the pride of having a good looking "rig," or cart. White on the chest however, was not only allowed, but thought by some breeders to be an indication of intelligence and willingness to work. The work noted that the herding dogs, whose value was only based on how they worked in the field with stock, included a wide variety of colors which are no longer part of the Rottweiler breed today.

Written sources from the First World War place the height around twenty-four inches for dogs, twenty-one and a half for bitches. This is about an inch taller than a separate source dating back to the early 1880's, but about two inches shorter than the present day breed. The weight was fifty-four to sixty-one pounds, forty-five to fifty-seven pounds for bitches, which is a dog about half the weight of the present day breed.

The breed obviously has changed considerably in the last eighty years. Heads have become broader and muzzles shorter than was evident at the turn of the century. The dogs have become heavier, blockier and more heavily boned. (More substance is how a breeder might refer to the changes.) But you will still see a wide variety of head style and bone weight within the breed, as not all breeders are as eager and quick to embrace the new look as others. The dog today is probably more like the original draft dog version than the herding version, and has considerably influenced from mastiff-like breeds such as the Boxer and the Bulldog.

At the same time, the Rottweiler has maintained his intelligence, all-around ability, agility, and enthusiasm for work. These are the qualities which have attracted so many supporters. The Rottweiler is very agile for a dog of his weight and size, surprisingly quick, and able to jump with ease, hence his success in the obedience and agility rings. He is successful in carting competitions, and is an excellent Schutzhund and police dog.

From his earliest days he has been a dog who lived and worked with his family, played with the children, and developed a strong family loyalty. The "Good Dog Carl" personality is very much a part of the breed, and a strong tradition held over from its German roots. In fact, the books of *Good Dog Carl* are modern remakes of a long out-of-print book found in a German antique store by the present American authors! There are many outstanding therapy Rottweilers, and many who have been successful in various handicapped programs.

ROTTWEILERS AROUND THE WORLD

The Rottweiler has had enormous success in the United States and in Great Britain. They are one of the most popular breeds in the world, though they are not always the same from country to country.

Rottweilers were imported to Australia, but were slow to become popular there. Their foundation stock came from Great Britain after the war, with several more imported in 1962. In the late 1980's, a very fine dog was imported from Germany, and his blood flows in some wonderful dogs throughout that country. Today, there are a large number of Rottweilers in Australia. The Rottweiler was late in arriving in New Zealand, where the first Rottweiler arrived only in 1970. Most of the dogs in New Zealand today came from the U.K. and Australia. Dog shows in Australia and New Zealand are very informal compared to those in the United States; the

Though relatively new as a recognized breed, the Rottweiler has become very popular around the world.

entries are much smaller in number, and the day is a festive chance to show dogs, swap stories, drink beer and have a get together of dog people while showing some fine dogs. For this, the Rottweiler seems to be perfectly suited.

South Africa imported Rottweilers as early as the 1930's, but they were not common until the 1970's. During the 70's, the breed grew in popularity until it became one of the more prevalent breeds in that country. Many dogs in South Africa do not show, but live in rural areas doing much of the same kind of work they did in Germany for centuries.

Most of the South African dogs came directly from Europe, Holland and Germany specifically, since there are no quarantine restrictions into that country as there are in England and Australia.

Of course there are a number of dogs throughout Europe, including Denmark, Sweden and Finland. Germany, the country of origin, continues to play an important role in the breed throughout the world. The German club continues to endeavor to control the breed throughout the world, though breeders and breed clubs in England and the United States have proven to be very independent. British and American breeders have shown their ability to produce quality dogs using their own criteria and methods.

Rottweilers are particularly popular in many of the Caribbean countries. There are several popular international dog shows in the Bahamas, Jamaica and other island nations. Many of the dogs in our Hall of Fame carry championship or obedience titles from these island countries. These titles are indicated by the abbreviation of the country in front of the title. There is a large and very competitive group of Rottweiler breeders who enjoy meeting the international competition.

In less than thirty years, the Rottweiler has gone from a relatively small breed to one which has become popular throughout the world.

SHOULD YOU BUY A ROTTWEILER?

*B*efore you consider buying a Rottweiler, decide if you are ready to buy a dog at all. If this is a first dog for the family, or for yourself, remember that dogs, unlike fish and cats, need your time as you raise them, care for them, exercise them and socialize them. Training is a must for a dog as large as a Rottweiler. You will have expenses beyond the original investment, such as vet bills and dog food. If you leave on vacation, you will have to provide care for the dog. At this point is should be mentioned that it is often less expensive to invest more money initially and buy a dog from a reputable breeder. In the long run you will probably save money in vet bills, training, or in damages trying to overcome a poor temperament. Paying $1,000 for a good dog, which will live ten years, means that you are investing about $8 a month to own a good Rottweiler, which is less than it will cost you to feed him!

Rottweilers are smart dogs, and they enjoy a wide range of activities. They are used for police work, guarding, herding, companions and even as therapy and guide dogs. To achieve success with your Rottweiler, you will need to dedicate time to his training; emotional energy to his well being and socialization; training for any children you have in the house on how to handle and respect a dog and his rights; and enough money to ensure he has proper facilities, food and health care. Consistency is the key to training any dog, especially a Rottweiler. And patience is needed to get through the puppy stage and ensure that you emerge with a confident, well adjusted adult. Without time and training, a Rottweiler may well use his intelligence in ways which damage your property, or he may use the excess time he has to concentrate on escaping his living quarters. In the back yard, he may spend time investigating things which are better left alone. An unsupervised dog with time on his paws, will almost certainly become more of a problem in your life than a joy to the family.

After you have decided that you have the time, energy, and money to make the initial investment and to take on the commitment of a dog, take a good look at your living situation. How many members are there in your family? Who is going to be responsible for the daily care and feeding? Do all the members of the family want a dog, and can they all agree on what kind of dog they want? If the wife wants a quiet, small dog and the kids want a playful, large dog, there are bound to be conflicts ahead. What kind of space do you have? Is there a fenced yard? If not, how will the dog get exercise and where will he stay when the family is at work or at school? Where will the dog sleep? What rooms of the house will he have access to?

Housing is an important issue. A Rottweiler is a large, strong dog. He will need a yard fenced with a stout, six foot fence. He should have a shelter of his own outside, and a place in the house where he can be with the family. A crate is essential for nights until he is well trained, and even as an adult, a crate will make him a better traveler when he goes on vacation with the family. (See the chapter on Shipping and Travel.) Most of our breeders recommended crates for puppies and we will discuss their use in the training chapter.

Many of our breeders suggested that you make decisions on what rules you expect the dog to live by. For example, will he be allowed to get on the sofa if the family is watching T.V.? Will he be taught to sit and obey, or will he simply be allowed to do as he pleases? Will he be allowed to be in the house most of the day, or will he be expected to stay outside? Will he be traveling with the family?

Decide ahead of time what qualities you want in a dog. Will he be expected to guard the house and defend the family? What kind of neighborhood do you live in? How often will he *really* be required to act as a guard dog?

Then take a look at various breeds. One of our breeders said she gets very angry when a caller inquires about the difference between a Labrador and a Rottweiler. There are almost no similarities except for the basic color black and four legs! They are two different breeds, with very different personalities and temperaments. And they will serve a different purpose within the family or household.

Do your homework about breeds. Find out what the breed is like from talking to several breeders, but be sure that you have intelligent questions to ask before you begin. You will get much more appreciation and respect from breeders if you have taken the time to look into the breed before you call.

The American Rottweiler Club (ARC) is very perturbed by the number of unscrupulous people who are breeding and selling Rottweilers. In an effort to safeguard prospective buyers against those who would sell animals of inferior quality and/or unstable temperament, frequently at inflated prices, the ARC urges buyers to consider *before* they *buy*.

The temperament of the Rottweiler should be calm, confident and courageous. This ***does not mean snappy or aggressive***. The Rottweiler has an inherent desire to protect home and family, and is intelligent and adaptable, with a hardness about him and a willingness to work. ***Shy, timid or mindlessly aggressive dogs are not acceptable.*** Do not expect a puppy to show aggressive traits. Aggressiveness in a pup often means an unwillingness to get along with littermates, and occasionally people, who resist the pup. This kind of pup will likely grow up to be difficult to deal with, especially with other pets.

The breed grows to be 24 inches to twenty-seven inches tall, with bitches 22 to 25 inches. The preference is for a dog or bitch in the middle of the size range. They will weigh 95 to 135 pounds for dogs, with bitches 80 to 100 pounds. Rottweilers will live to be about ten years old.

Their temperaments vary from the natural clown who is affectionate to almost anyone, to the very reserved, one-person dog. If you have evaluated your home, you should have some idea of the type of temperament you want before you purchase. Make your preference known to the breeder, who is used to looking at his pups from an early age and will likely be able to spot the type of personality you want for your situation. With such a range in temperament, you can be in for an unpleasant living situation if you are looking for a clown who will love children and you get a one-person dog which is reserved. Ideally the Rottweiler should be a calm but alert companion. Rotts often follow their master from place to place in the home, keeping a constant but unobtrusive watch over their loved ones. Nervous, shy, excitable or hyperactive dogs are exhibiting traits which are undesirable in an animal the size and nature of the Rottweiler and should be avoided.

Aggressiveness is a trait which varies with the indi-

For their size and bulk, Rottweilers are very energetic and agile. They love to jump and play in a variety of different activities.

vidual dog to some degree, although all have a strong territorial instinct and will defend their master's home, car and property from intruders. Rottweilers have also been known to bully or bluff their owners or other people, a trait which you must be prepared to cope with before you buy a Rottweiler. A strong personality on the part of the owner, and early obedience training, should lead to a mutually rewarding working relationship between the owner and the dog.

The protective instinct is the reason many families have purchased a Rottweiler, only to discover that it brings with it a considerable moral and legal responsibility. Problems can arise quickly; the dog may not be able to distinguish between a bear hug greeting of a family member or a cherished friend and a hostile advance of an intruder, particularly if the greeting between parties includes loud shouts, laughter or screams. Dogs must be carefully schooled to accept your friends and other people who will enter your home. Physical contact must be approached carefully until the dog realizes that the person is a welcome member of the home. Strangers must never come into your yard unannounced. The dog doesn't know the difference between family friends looking to borrow the lawnmower and a burglar going into the garage. Delivery persons or neighbors in the yard in the owner's absence may end up cornered or very unnerved. Make sure that deliveries are made either when you are home, by people familiar with the dog, or when the dog is contained inside the house or in a secure place.

The Rottweiler is a working breed, and is often happiest when he is given a chance to work. Take the time to work with your dog, to give him a job to do, and to give him the training he needs to be a contributing member of your family. It is *very necessary* to establish control of the animal from the very beginning. ***This does not mean through force, abuse or violence.*** This kind of "training" will almost certainly do nothing but bring out a defensive, aggressive temperament. Physical mastery of the dog is generally less important than sensitive, patient and positive training methods. Women have been very successful with the Rottweiler and patience is an important factor.

Sensitive and intelligent, the Rottweiler usually wants to please. But there are times when the dog can be quite stubborn and these times require more attention and a firm physical correction. Ownership is not for the timid person, or one who has a very busy schedule and little time or patience to spend with the dog.

If you have small children in the home, you will need to be sure of two things. First, talk to your breeder. Although some Rottweilers are wonderful babysitters and have infinite patience with a toddler, others resent the rough treatment by the child. It is of utmost importance that you select a dog from a reputable breeder who has placed emphasis on temperament if you mean to put the dog into this kind of situation. Second, *train your child early and well on the handling of the dog.* Toddlers can sometimes be quite abusive and rough with a dog. Be as consistent with the child as you are with the dog, watching carefully for harsh behavior, and saying "No" to the child, putting a stop to the tempestuous treatment as soon as possible. Teaching a child respect for living creatures not only develops a desirable behavior pattern, but it may prevent a serious accident, if not with your dog, with some neighborhood dog at a later time.

One problem which is difficult to overcome is the sheer size of the dog. A small baby or child may be injured inadvertently when the dog bumps into him or knocks him over in play. A well behaved dog and a well supervised child are the best combination and assurance that all will live together in harmony. The "bumping" instinct is natural for the Rottweiler, dating back to the time when he was used as a herding dog and physically bumped into cattle to control the stubborn beasts. This can also be a problem if you have elderly people in the home. Some breeders recommend waiting to purchase a Rottweiler until children are of school age. Other breeders were enthusiastic about the Rottweiler with children, even those of a very young age. One of our breeders suggested that German import lines had a tendency to be more aggressive than the lines which have been in the United States for many generations. She suggested looking for strong, sound temperamented American lines if you have children in the family. We suggest you discuss this point with your breeder carefully before you buy a puppy if you have young children.

Decide what sex you are looking for. Consider that a full grown male may be a little more aggressive toward other animals, and other male dogs in particular, but a female will have mood swings with her heat cycle and an aggressive bitch will often be aggressive toward other bitches, males and animals in general. **Neutered and spayed dogs or bitches have the most stable personalities, and there are many health reasons to spay and neuter animals which are not being bred.** *Most people interested in dogs and their welfare, from breeders to the SPCA, strongly recommend spaying or neutering.* Talk to your breeder extensively about which sex would be best for your home situation before you arbitrarily decide on one sex or the other. Sometimes there is a difference in price between genders based on popular demand and this may vary from breeder to breeder. Also tell your if breeder you intend to spay or neuter your dog. While most breeders enthusiastically endorse this practice, a breeder may not want to "lose" that particular dog from future breeding programs they have in mind.

Frequently people with new families will want to raise a puppy with the baby. But the caregiver for the baby may be taxed to the limit and may not be anxious to take on another living being. An older dog, one which has already had some training, may be an excellent choice. Often show breeders keep a dog to see how it will turn out for show purposes. Sometimes they will keep two brothers, or a son when they already own the sire, to see which will be the more successful. Show breeders are always looking for a bigger winner. When a dog fails to meet the potential the breeder hoped it would have, the breeder

often seeks to place the dog in a good home. These dogs are excellent buys, since they are usually lovely examples of the breed, and they already have good solid training and socialization (often under extreme circumstances such as strange people, loud noises and general confusion). They are usually housetrained and crate trained, and know how to behave and have a mastery of basic commands. Also, with an adult dog, you already know the traits and characteristics of the individual, along with his faults and any health problems.

If you have other pets or dogs in the home, a Rottweiler puppy will probably adjust easily. An older dog, however, may have a more difficult time adjusting to a new situation which includes another dog, a cat or some other animal. Early socialization makes a difference in dog-to-dog aggression later in life, so an older dog will be influenced by early experience. It is also influenced, however, by sex, bloodline, and the individual dog's personality, so it is sometimes possible to get a puppy, have him adjust well to a cat or other small animal, and later have problems when the dog matures. Males are less tolerant of other males than they are of females. However, one of our breeders noted that two males have shared her house for years without a problem. It is difficult to know exactly what type of personality a puppy will have when it grows up since not only bloodlines will influence the attitude, but also early experiences, the personality of the owner and the dog's training will play a part. Bitches may also be intolerant of other dogs, sometimes of either sex, though as a general rule bitches will be more tolerant of dogs than of other bitches. The best recommendation is early obedience training and getting the puppy out in public places and around other dogs from the beginning of his or her life.

A Rottweiler's destructive tendencies will vary with age, training, temperament and activity level of the individual. Digging, chewing, fence climbing, jumping and other destructive habits will be more likely in puppies and young adults (under two years of age), than in an older, more mature dog. Lots of attention, socialization and interaction with people, obedience training and regular workouts can help. A dog which is left alone for long periods of time, bored and without regular exercise which will reduce his energy level, is likely to be hard on landscaping, furniture, trees and personal property. Never leave a dog alone with chew toys or loose beds, since the powerful jaws can shred these items quickly and parts may be swallowed, causing the dog to choke.

Many of our breeders recommended a crate to contain the dog in a safe environment while the owner is away. Dogs like crates once they have gotten used to them. A crate is a dog's home. It smells like him, and it gives the comfort of the cave. Use of a crate will not only help with early housetraining, but it will also help keep the owner happy because the house stays intact, and the dog is safe from possible hazards while the owner is away. Keep in mind that the Rottweiler is a large dog, with large powerful jaws and strong legs. Not only can those jaws and paws do damage to a great many things, from table legs, to electric cords, to shoes, but the dog's size allows him to reach counters and table tops when standing on his hind legs.

Fencing is another issue. Because of the size and activity level of some Rottweilers, strong, secure fencing is a *must*. Most breeders will ask if you have a fenced yard before they will sell you a dog. Secure gate latches and stout fencing are important. The jaws of a Rottweiler are strong enough to literally eat through many of the lighter gauge, inexpensive chain link runs which are sold at local discount stores. Fencing should be a full six feet in height. The Rottweiler is very agile for his size and weight, and although some of them have little inclination to jump, others will jump for exercise or simply to see if they can. Covered runs are suggested for jumpers. One of our breeders recommended a standard livestock electric fence around the top edge if the run is an odd shape, or too large to accommodate a covered top. Anchor fencing securely with stakes extending into the ground to prevent digging underneath.

If your backyard is frequently invaded by strangers such as a pool man or a gardener, be sure that the dog has a separate fenced area. If the puppy gets used to a person from the time he is young, that may be fine until a new gardener or worker replaces the individual who has gained the dog's confidence. Many times owners do not realize that it is the person the dog has adjusted to, not the fact that a stranger is in the backyard. Failure to recognize this when a new person is expected to enter the yard can be disastrous. Part of responsible Rottweiler ownership is recognition of this type of potential problem.

Rottweilers should never be staked out on a chain for exercise. One of our breeders

has written her contract to state that if the dog is tied up she has a right to reclaim the dog from the new owner. A chained Rottweiler is a sure prescription for an ill-tempered, ill mannered dog. If that is your only way of containing a dog, don't buy any dog, especially not a Rottweiler. Rottweilers have been kept successfully in large apartments, but many breeders suggest getting an older dog if that is your situation. Puppies and young adults need exercise and access to the outdoors on a fairly regular basis. Daily exercise in the form of walks, jogging, playing ball or other fairly rigorous activity is a must if the dog is to live in a small house or apartment. If you don't have the time to exercise a Rottweiler, or you don't have space for a yard, consider a smaller, less active breed. Remember, a Rottweiler, just like any other breed, is not for everyone, or every living situation. You may find however, that although owning a Rottweiler requires commitment in terms of time and training, the bonding between dog and owner is personal and rewarding. Many owners prefer to exercise their dogs by hand rather than letting them run alone in the back yard because they enjoy the time spent with the animal and the companionship between the dog and master.

Like most heavy breeds with short muzzles, cooling air into the Rottweiler's lungs is not as efficient as in a breed with a long, slender nose such as sight hounds. The Rottweiler is also dark in color, and like all black dogs he tolerates cold better than heat. Be sure that there is adequate shelter and shade in the summer if temperatures climb; if you live in a very hot part of the country, some kind of shelter with a fan and good air circulation is necessary to prevent heat stroke. Direct sun on the black coat will almost certainly spell disaster and a dog can overheat and die of heat stroke even when the temperature is not much more than 90 degrees if there is no shelter or shade. Be sure that the dog has ready access to water at all times in the summer. A bowl of cold water in the summer is a nice treat, and one your dog will appreciate. When you travel, always be sure you have a thermos of cold water.

Colder weather is not a problem in all but the most severe conditions. The thick coat and heavy body structure keep these rugged mountain dogs comfortable in most cold climates as long as adequate shelter is provided. Our breeders report that Rottweilers will play endlessly in the snow. But the Rottweiler functions best in contact with his family, and outside shelter always away from people is never a good solution.

A Rottweiler will consume from ten to fifteen pounds of good quality kibble each week. This will run about $30 - $35 per month. Puppies will consume amazing amounts of dog food because they grow very rapidly. Combined with regular veterinary health care such as worming and shots, the cost of owning a Rottweiler is somewhere around $50 per month. Additional costs such as spaying and neutering; maintenance of fencing; supplies such as bedding, crates, and other items which will make your life and your dog's life easier; and the cost of obedience classes (which are *highly recommended*) can run the cost of owning a dog up another several hundred dollars a year.

The American Rottweiler Club, most reputable breeders, and certainly the editorial staff of this book urge you to investigate carefully before you buy a Rottweiler. A reputable breeder is one who is breeding dogs of sound, stable temperaments, who are healthy and physically sound, and whose lines are free of genetic defects.

The correct color for a Rottweiler is **black with rust or mahogany markings**. If you see an advertisement for any other color, *be aware that this is certainly a rare color, but it is also undesirable*! Dogs of any color except black and rust or mahogany cannot be shown, should **never** be bred, and are probably being bred by a breeder who is either ignorant or unethical. Efforts are being made by the National Rottweiler Club to make these dogs ineligible for registration. If you are buying a mismarked dog from a reputable breeder (and they do occasionally turn up in good pedigrees), the breeder will probably give you limited registration papers (see the chapter on Paperwork), insist that you neuter or spay the dog, and will certainly be up front about the fact that this is an undesirable color.

Finally, temperament is critical in the Rottweiler. The dog should be calm, confident and courageous. Although he has a strong, natural desire to protect his home, he should not be aggressive or mindless in his challenge of authority. Likewise, shy, timid or nervous dogs are also undesirable. Shy dogs often become fear biters, a dangerous and difficult behavior to deal with. Training based on consistency and control are of primary importance if you are interested in owning a Rottweiler, and you must be willing to devote the time and energy this will take before you undertake to buy a puppy. Buying a Rottweiler should *never* be an impulsive decision!

The price of a quality Rottweiler will range from $500 or $600 for a pet and $1,500 or more for a show dog. Remember that the puppy or adult is priced by the quality of the

dog, not by the purpose for which you will use it, so if you want a really nice dog, with no major show faults and good bone and head, you will be looking at a show potential puppy whether you intend to show it or not — and the price will be higher than if you are willing to accept some faults which may put the dog firmly into the pet category. Bad bites, large white spots on the stomach or chest, cryptorchid or unilateral cryptorchid (males without one or both testicles, which should make no difference to you if you are seeking a pet, since pets should be neutered), light eyes, long or curling hair, or bad ears or ear carriage are some of the most common reasons for a puppy to be considered a pet.

Some of these faults will make little or no difference to a pet owner. Many dogs with improper bites are perfectly able to eat, maintain body weight and live normal lives. No one will ever see the alignment of the teeth except the vet, so the dog is not noticeably anything but a lovely specimen. Other faults, however, will change the look of the dog. Light eyes, for example, may or may not bother you. They do change the expression, and dark eyes are correct for the breed. That change in expression may not make a difference to some owners, yet it may make the dog unattractive to others. The same is true for lighter bone or sharper heads — both frequent reasons for a dog to be a pet. Probably less likely to bother a pet owner is a white spot on the stomach. Be sure to ask the breeder *why* a dog is being sold as a pet, and consider carefully if the particular fault or faults the dog has will bother you, or even be evident to you. Some faults are things which a show breeder or judge would notice (such as improper shoulder structure or a back which is not quite level), but you would probably never recognize. These are

A Rottweiler working sheep. The herding instinct which once was necessary in the Butcher's Dog is still present in the modern Rottweiler.

structural things which anyone involved in breeding and showing the breed will see automatically, but someone who is not used to seeing and evaluating show dogs would probably have a hard time understanding even if it was pointed out to them. Breeders and judges take years to develop this "eye for a dog."

These are all things to consider *before* you purchase any dog. Consider the space in your home, the family and its members, how much time you can give a dog, what you want the dog to do within the family, how attractive you wish the dog to be and if you want a dog which is under your feet all the time or off on its own until you wish to interact with it. How much time will each member of the family spend with the dog and how differently do you expect the dog to behave under different circumstances? Do you have the money to spend on the dog, both in the purchase and the upkeep?

Sometimes people begin with a dog for a pet, and later become interested in showing, obedience, working competitions or agility. (We will talk more about these activities you can enjoy with your dog in the chapter on Dog Shows and Other Competitions.) A second dog may be the answer. Several good kennels began with a pet, got interested in competition, and ended up purchasing another dog for that specific purpose. If you are thinking about using your dog for competitions, you will enjoy seeing some of the top winners we have featured in the Hall of Fame and doing some further investigating on your own. You will see that Rottweilers are outstanding competitors in a wide variety of activities.

THE STANDARD

*T*he standard is very important to breeders because it gives them something written against which to measure their dogs. Unlike dog shows, where the judge bases his decision on what is the best dog being presented to him from the entries showing that day, the standard describes the ideal dog of a breed. Without a written standard describing what the breed should look like, a breed would change freely at the whim of what was popular with judges and breeders at the time. In a few generations the breed would look completely different. The standard pulls the breed back to the middle of the range, but individual dogs will vary in some ways. In fact, there is seldom, if ever, a dog which meets the standard perfectly. Breeding with the standard in mind is one thing that marks the difference between "Good Breeders," "Puppy Mills," and uneducated "Backyard Breeders." Breeders who take the time and trouble to learn their breed, to evaluate their dogs, and to make informed breedings which will keep their puppies in the range where they are still easily recognizable as their breed are those who best insure the future of the Rottweiler.

Many times pet owners will ask why it is important to them if the breeder breeds to the standard. The reason is quite obvious. If, as a new owner, you have taken the time to look into the breed, to select one which fits your family and your needs, and one whose appearance is pleasing to you, and you purchase a puppy based on that decision, you have the right to a dog which will grow up and be recognizable as that breed. As long as a dog has AKC papers, and it is bred to a bitch with AKC papers, and the paperwork is in order, AKC will issue papers for puppies. But that does not ensure that those puppies will indeed grow up to be representative of their breed. For that, you must trust your breeder and his knowledge of the breed standard.

Every breed which shows anywhere in the world has a written Standard of the Breed by which the dog is judged. This standard is important in preserving "breed type," or in layman's terms, those characteristics which make a Rottweiler a Rottweiler and not a Labrador Retriever!

The Standard is written by the breed club in the country, usually heavily based on the standard from the country of origin. The standard may sometimes vary from country to country, though it is generally very similar since it describes the same breed.

"Style" is how the individual dog looks. Although the dog is easy to recognize as a Rottweiler for example, and he fits the standard, there are always words and phrases which are subject to interpretation. Breeders and judges may disagree on exactly what the standard means by placing different emphasis on different words and phrases. This leads to slight differences in the look of the individual dog from country to country, from one geographic location to another within the United States, and even between kennels. We suggest you take a good look at the "Hall of Fame" section. Look at the different dogs and try to see the difference in looks, or "style," between them. Then look at the pedigrees beneath the pictures. Are there similar names in the pedigrees of the dogs you like? See if you can identify why some of the dogs will be more appealing to you than others. All of the dogs pictured in the Hall of Fame are outstanding dogs of their breed. They have earned the right to be in this section. But, because of the difference in interpretation of the breed standard, and the different purposes for which the breeder wishes his dogs to be used, there will be differences between dogs in what is referred to as "style."

The standard for the Rottweiler was changed in accordance with the new AKC format, approved by AKC in May of 1990, and went into effect in June of 1990 as the standard by which the breed is judged. It reads as follows:

GENERAL APPEARANCE — The ideal Rottweiler is a medium large, robust and powerful dog, black with clearly defined rust markings. His compact and substantial build denotes great strength, agility and endurance. Dogs are characteristically more massive throughout with larger frame and heavier bone than bitches. Bitches are distinctly feminine, but without weakness of substance or structure.

SIZE, PROPORTION, & SUBSTANCE — Dogs - 24 inches to 27 inches. Bitches - 22 inches to 25 inches, with preferred size being mid-range of each sex. Correct proportion is of primary importance, as long as size is within the standard's range. The length of body, from prosternum to the rear most projection of the rump, is slightly longer than the height of the dog at the withers, the most desirable proportion of the height to length being 9 to 10. The Rottweiler is neither coarse nor shelly. Depth of chest is approximately fifty percent (50%) of the height of the dog. His bone and muscle mass must be sufficient to balance his frame, giving a compact and very powerful appearance. Serious faults - Lack of proportion, undersized, oversized, reversal of sex characteristics (bitchy dogs, doggy bitches).

HEAD — Of medium length, broad between the ears; forehead line seen in profile is moderately arched; zygomatic arch and stop well developed with strong broad upper and lower jaws. The desired ratio of backskull to muzzle is 3 to 2. Forehead is preferred dry, however some wrinkling may occur when the dog is alert. **Expression** is noble, alert and self-assured. **Eyes** of medium size, almond shaped with well fitting lids, moderately deep-set, neither protruding nor receding. The desired color is a uniform dark brown. Serious Faults - Yellow (bird of prey) eyes, eyes of different color or size, hairless eye rim. Disqualification - Entropion, Ectropion. **Ears** of medium size, pendant, triangular in shape; when carried alertly the ears are level with the top of the skull and appear to broaden it. Ears are to be set well apart, hanging forward with the inner edge lying tightly against the head and terminating at approximately mid-cheek. Serious Faults - Improper carriage (creased, folded or held away from cheek/head.) **Muzzle** - Bridge is straight, broad at base with slight tapering towards tip. The end of the muzzle is broad with well developed chin. Nose is broad rather than round and always black. **Lips -** Always black; corners closed; inner mouth pigment is preferred dark. Serious Fault - Total lack of mouth pigment (pink mouth). **Bite and Dentition -** Teeth 42 in number (20 upper, 22 lower), strong, correctly placed, meeting in a scissor bite - lower incisors touching inside of upper incisors. Serious Faults - Level bite; any missing tooth. Disqualifications - Overshot, undershot (when incisors do not touch or mesh; wry mouth; two or more missing teeth.

NECK, TOPLINE, BODY — **Neck -** Powerful, well muscled, moderately long, slightly arched and without loose skin. **Topline -** The back is firm and level, extending in a straight line from behind the withers to the croup. The back remains horizontal to the ground while the dog is moving or standing. **Body -** The chest is roomy, broad and deep, reaching to elbow, with well pronounced forechest and well sprung, oval ribs. Back is straight and strong. Loin is short, deep and well muscled. Croup is broad, of medium length and only slightly sloping. Underline of mature Rottweiler has a slight tuck-up. Males must have two normal testicles properly descended into the scrotum. Disqualifications -Unilateral cryptorchid or cryptorchid males. **Tail -** Tail docked short, close to body, leaving one or two tail vertebrae. The set of the tail is more important than length. Properly set, it gives an impression of elongation of topline; carried slightly above horizontal when the dog is excited or moving.

FOREQUARTERS — Shoulder blade is long and well laid back. Upper arm equal in length to shoulder blade, set so elbows are well under body. Distance from withers to elbow and elbow to ground is equal. Legs are strongly developed with straight, heavy bone, not set close together. Pasterns are strong, springy and almost perpendicular to ground. Feet are round, compact with well arched toes, turning neither in nor out. Pads are thick and hard. Nails short, strong and black. Dewclaws may be removed.

HINDQUARTERS — Angulation of hindquarters balances that of forequarters. Upper thigh is fairly long, very broad and well muscled. Stifle joint is well turned. Lower thigh is long, broad and powerful, with extensive muscling leading into a strong hock joint. Rear pasterns are nearly perpendicular to the ground. Viewed from the rear, hind legs are straight, strong and wide enough apart to fit with a properly built body. Feet are somewhat longer than the front feet, turning neither in nor out, equally compact with well arched toes. Pads are thick and hard. Nails short, strong and black. Dewclaws must be removed.

COAT — Outer coat is straight, coarse, dense of medium length and lying flat. Undercoat should be present on neck and thighs, but the amount is influenced by climatic conditions. Undercoat should not show through outer coat. The coat is shortest on head, ears and legs, longest on breeching. The Rottweiler is to be exhibited in the natural condition with no trimming. Fault - Wavy coat. Serious Faults - Open, excessively short, or curly coat; total lack of undercoat; any trimming that alters the length of the natural coat. Disqualification - Long coat.

COLOR - Always black with rust to mahogany markings. The demarcation between black and rust is to be clearly defined. The markings should be located as follows: a spot over each eye; on cheeks; as a strip around each side of muzzle, but not on the bridge of the nose; on throat; triangular mark on both sides of posternum; on forelegs from carpus downward to the toes; on inside of rear legs showing down the front of the stifle and broadening out to front of rear legs from hock to toes, but not completely eliminating black from rear of pasterns; under tail; black penciling on toes. The undercoat is gray, tan or black. Quantity and location of rust marking is important and should not exceed ten percent of body color. Serious Faults - Straw colored, excessive, insufficient or sooty markings; rust marking other than described above; white marking any place on dog (a few rust or white hairs do not constitute a marking). Disqualifications - any base color other than black; absence of all markings.

GAIT - The Rottweiler is a trotter. His movement should be balanced, harmonious, sure, powerful and unhindered, with strong forereach and a powerful rear drive. The motion is effortless, efficient and ground-covering. Front and rear legs are thrown neither in nor out, as the imprint of hind feet should touch that of forefeet. In a trot the forequarters and hindquarters are mutually coordinated while the back remains level, firm and relatively motionless. As speed increases the legs will converge under body towards a center line.

TEMPERAMENT — The Rottweiler is basically a calm, confident and courageous dog with a self-assured aloofness that does not lend itself to immediate and indiscriminate friendships. A Rottweiler is self-confident and responds quietly and with a wait-and-see attitude to influences in his environment. He has an inherent desire to protect home and family, and is an intelligent dog of extreme hardness and adaptability with a strong willingness to work, making him especially suited as a companion, guardian and general all purpose dog.

The behavior of the Rottweiler in the show ring should be controlled, willing and adaptable, trained to submit to examination of mouth, testicles, etc. An aloof or reserved dog should not be penalized, as this reflects the accepted character of the breed. An aggressive or belligerent attitude towards other dogs should not be faulted.

A judge shall excuse from the ring any shy Rottweiler. A dog shall be judged fundamentally shy if, refusing to stand for examination, it shrinks away from the judge.

A dog that in the opinion of the judge menaces or threatens him/her, or exhibits any sign that it may not be safely approached or examined by the judge in the normal manner, shall be excused from the ring. A dog that in the opinion of the judge attacks any person in the ring shall be disqualified.

FAULTS - The foregoing is a description of the ideal Rottweiler. Any structural fault that detracts from the above described working dog must be penalized to the extent of the deviation.

DISQUALIFICATIONS - Entropion, ectropion. Overshot, undershot (where incisors do not touch or mesh); wry mouth; two or more missing teeth. Unilateral cryptorchid or cryptorchid males. Long coat. Any base color other than black; absence of all markings. A dog that in the opinion of the judge attacks any person in the ring.

All of this is a very complex way of describing what a Rottweiler should look like, and why it does not look like any other breed. Some of the terms used are historical, such as the description of the expression as being "noble, alert and self-assured." Other terms are specific for dog show judging, or are widely accepted terms in judging animals. When the Standard refers to "doggy" bitches or "bitchy" dogs, all judges, or people involved in dog breeding, understand what that means. It refers to a fine boned male with a sweet expression, or a very large, coarse looking female. There are supposed to be differences between the sexes in the Rottweiler, and a confusion of males with females is to be avoided. Other terms refer to specific parts of the dog such as "zygomatic arch and stop." This description of the head means that part of the head behind the eyes and in front of the ears and neck (zygomatic arch), and the slope between the eyes which connects the muzzle with the top of the head (stop). "Withers" and "croup" are terms which describe body parts of most animals, from dogs and horses to sheep and cattle. The withers are the shoulders; the croup is the area from the hip to the tail.

For a breeder of quality dogs, the Standard is his blueprint for breeding future generations to ensure that each generation will indeed be clearly recognizable as a Rottweiler.

If you are going to take the time to decide on a breed, to find a breeder and to purchase a puppy or adult of that breed, it should have the characteristics of that breed. If it does not, you might as well have saved your time and money, as any crossbreed would have done just as well as a purebred which is so poor that it does not carry the typical characteristics of its breed.

In layman's terms, this Standard describes a dog whose back will be about mid-thigh on the average adult. The weight will be equal to that of a trim adult woman. The Rottweiler should be stocky looking, almost as tall as it is long, with a broad back and sturdy legs. It has strong bones, a broad head with a short, broad muzzle that should NOT come to a point. The head should be set on a short, thick neck. The back is level, and the tail is short. The dog should not be clumsy looking, nor lean looking. It should move with a powerful, easy gait.

It is important to know that the standard is not something you will need to know if you have simply bought a nice pet from a good breeder. Your dog, because of his genetic heritage, will look like his breed, and his breeder will be able to tell you exactly where he deviates from the standard, and what makes him a pet. If you buy a dog from someone who does NOT know the standard, however, the chances are that the breeding has not been done with the ideal dog in mind, and the puppy produced may not look anything like the dog we have described above, or what you have in mind when you picture a Rottweiler. Before you consider breeding your dog, you will need to learn the standard, learn how it applies to dogs, yours in particular, learn how to evaluate the strengths and weaknesses in your bitch or dog, and seek out a mate which will be strong where your animal is weak, thus pulling the puppies back toward the standard for the breed.

When you talk to a breeder, he should be able to tell you both about the standard and how his dogs compare. Remember, there is no dog which perfectly matches the standard, but it is important for a breeder to know his dogs well.

"Style" is another thing which will affect a breeding or a kennel. Some terms in the standard are very specific and do not allow for any interpretation. The size is stated in terms of inches, and is easy to measure. But one breeder may find an outstanding dog which is either above or below the size stated in the standard, and may still use him for breeding because he may have an outstanding head, good proportion, and be an excellent mover with strong OFA hips. Another breeder may see the same dog, focus on the size, and refuse to use him for breeding because in that one respect, he does not meet the exact size requirements of the standard. This is because some breeders will look at the overall dog, and if it is especially nice or has a look which that breeder feels is especially good for the breed, they will use the dog for breeding even if it has a specific fault. Other breeders focus on the fault, and will use a dog which is not quite as nice overall but which does not have any specific faults. We will discuss this more in the chapter on showing.

Another factor affecting this is if the breeder feels his dogs are weak in one area and the dog with the fault is especially strong in that area. Thus, a breeder who feels his bitch is too straight in the rear legs may breed to a dog which is too large in size who has excellent angulation, especially if his bitch is on the smaller size of the standard. He will hope that some of the puppies at least will be the proper size with the sire's angulation in the rear, and he will accept that some of the puppies will be too large to be good show dogs. These oversized puppies will be pets. *No litter is all show dogs, no breeder produces all show dogs and no kennel has dogs which all meet the standard perfectly.* The joy and sport of breeding show dogs is the art of how close breeders can come to the standard, and how often.

Other terms, such as "moderately" arched forehead, "slightly" tapered muzzle, and "some wrinkling" on the forehead when the dog is alert, leave room for differences in opinion. Words like moderately, slightly and some, leave room for each breeder to decide just how much he or she will or will not accept.

Finally, style is affected by what part of the dog each breeder feels is most important. Some breeders select their stock based on a good head or neck. Some will place primary importance on movement. Debate will sometimes run high between breeders who feel that different things are of primary importance for the breed. When you look at the Hall of Fame, we have already mentioned that you will see differences between the dogs.

When you look at the pedigrees, and look back at the standard, you have taken your first lesson in what the sport of dog breeding involves, and why it produces dogs with certain common characteristics. This will explain why some breeders will get $500 for a puppy, while others will advertise in the newspaper and only ask $200. For $2.50 more a month over the lifetime of the dog, one puppy will give you pride and joy and will have the characteristics people have come to associate with the breed, and one may be only a poor imitation. It is no wonder that most reputable breeders have no trouble selling their puppies, while other litters of puppies may be in the paper week after week still looking for homes.

FINDING A BREEDER

*I*f you have the time, go to a local dog show and see Rottweilers in action. But don't expect to find puppies there. Good breeders — and AKC rules — keep puppies at home where they belong. It is sometimes difficult to talk to breeders at a show because they may be busy getting their dogs ready for the ring. Most show people take these events very seriously and therefore they may be short of small talk at the show. Remember that these exhibitors have a lot invested in the show at hand in terms of entry fees, travel and perhaps handling expenses and advertising. Selling you a puppy, or helping you to find one, is not likely to be their first priority.

However, a dog show is a good place to see different breeds in the ring and to compare the individuals of good quality with those you may have seen in your neighborhood. It is also a good place to find names and addresses of breeders. A catalog of the show will list the name of each dog, his sire and dam, the breeder and owner, and the date of birth. By watching the classes you can find dogs of the type and style you like and look up their owners. The address of the owner will be listed either with the entry, or in an index at the rear of the book. When you get home, call directory information for the number. Or write for information and a contact phone number.

Local kennel clubs may have a listing of breeders in your area. Calling breeders from some of the major dog publications is another way to begin finding a dog.

The role of a breeder is to preserve the breed into future generations. However, as we mentioned in the last chapter, every breeder will put emphasis on different qualities. Some kennels will breed for large bones or good heads, while others will feel that movement is the most important thing. Still others will put emphasis on temperament or health. This is not to say that every breeder doesn't want to breed lovely, sound, healthy dogs with wonderful temperaments, but they will select their breeding stock based on what they believe to be the most important thing first, and will sometimes accept a bitch or dog with a fault to get the things they feel are most important.

No dog is perfect! When a breeder starts to talk about his or her perfect dogs, RUN! The breeder is either a salesman or kennelblind — and neither is the kind of breeder you are looking for when you buy a pup. A salesman is only interested in making the sale and getting the money. The kennelblind breeder is not able to see why a particular dog might not fit *your* needs, even though it may be a good animal. What you need to know is what the breeder will accept in his or her breeding stock, and what will cause him to reject the dog completely. These differences between breeders will, after generations, make the difference between dogs from different kennels. When you look through the Hall of Fame, read what the breeder has to say. See if his purpose of breeding matches your needs. Talk with breeders long enough to know where they place emphasis, and what is not of great importance to them, and see how it matches your view of the breed, and what you want to use the dog for in your home. Then find a breeder with whom you agree and purchase a puppy from that breeder.

It is more important to find a breeder that you are comfortable with than to find one close to your home. Going to visit the litter may be fun, but it may also lead to buying a cute puppy which may not grow up to be the dog you really want. A good breeder, one who knows the bloodline and has watched the puppies from birth, will have a better idea of what will fit your lifestyle. Describe HOW you want the dog to fit into your household, what you expect it to do, and what your family is like. Ask the breeder how he or she feels on issues of importance to you. Listen carefully to the answers.

In the end, you are often better off trusting the breeder to select a puppy for your family than in picking it yourself. You will see the puppies for only a short time. They may all look alike to you, especially since the entire litter is the same color. One may be tired after a morning of playing, it may have just eaten and be sleepy, or it may have just awakened or be reacting to a littermate in an uncharacteristic way. The breeder has seen this litter for weeks, watching them and comparing them to other litters from the same bloodlines. They know more about each puppy from their past experience than you can possibly see within the framework of a short visit. Remember, the selection you make will be with you for many years and it should be based on sound judgment and as much information as possible before making the selection.

The Rottweiler is a very diverse breed. Not every Rottweiler will be equally good for every purpose. Temperament, size, style and bloodline will make a difference, especially if you have a particular purpose in mind, such as carting or obedience. There are a large number of obedience titled Rottweilers, and a growing number of owners and Rottweilers are very involved in carting — a long and honored tradition for the breed. There are many Rottweilers who are outstanding in Schutzhund work (more about this in the chapter on Dog Shows and Other Competitions), and some who have earned their titles in tracking. But not *every* dog will be equally suited to every task. This is one reason why it is important to decide *what* you want the dog to do *before* you begin to look for a puppy.

WHAT TO ASK A BREEDER

Be sure to identify the qualities you want in a dog. Because temperament varies within the breed, between kennels and between individuals, ask about how the breeder views the temperament of the breed in general, and this litter in particular. See how well the answers match your family and what you want in a pet. Don't seek conflicting qualities. An assertive guard dog may not be willing to accept kids, cats and other dogs. He is certainly *not* going to be a good dog if your home is frequented by guests coming and going, or a lot of extended family members who simply drop in.

Inquire about socialization. How have the pups been raised and what kind of temperaments have been noticed? If you have children, see if the line is good with children, either in the breeder's home or in other homes where the bloodline has been sold.

Ask the breeder what health problems may be in the breed. If the breeder continually states that there are no problems in health or temperament, no problems in training, and generally represents the dog as nothing but a 100% ideal pet, be careful. Bloodlines have their good points and their bad points. A good breeder will know both the strengths and weaknesses.

If you want a pet, ask *why* the dog is a pet then evaluate for yourself if the dog is a good buy. Many of the reasons for a dog to be classified as a pet are of no concern for the average pet owner. But if the dog is too light in bone and build to show, it will make a difference in the general appearance and may make it less appealing to you. If the coat is too long, that will change the appearance and may make a difference to you. Beware of breeders who claim that this is a perfect dog which just happens to be selling in a pet price range. But realize that a good breeder knows the value of his dogs, and years of experience have taught him what a fair value is for the pups he produces, even those with faults. Don't ever argue about why this pup is not worth the money because the breeder has been honest enough to admit a fault!

A pet puppy will begin at a price of $500 to $600, depending on the breeder and the puppy. Expect that the price will go up with the quality of the puppy. An especially cute puppy may run $700 to $1200. The breeder will price the puppy by how much he wants to keep the puppy for his own use as a breeding or show dog. Remember when talking about lower priced pups, the breeder has already taken into consideration that the pup has a fault and has priced him lower for that reason. A big boned pup with a nice head and a lot of white for example, may be priced at $500 because of his color. Don't assume that because there is a color fault the pup should be worth only $200! If this nice pup did not have the color fault he would be priced at $700 or more, depending on the kennel and the bloodline.

Likewise, if you want a good looking, top quality dog with an attractive head, large, solid bones and a level topline, you may be looking for a show quality dog, even if it is simply for a pet. In Rottweilers, bites (the way the teeth come together) are probably the most common reason for an otherwise lovely dog to be a pet. But bites cannot be determined for certain until the puppy is mature. Many of our breeders wrote that bites can go

off, or even come back into line as the dog matures. So, if this is the type of pet you are looking for, expect to find an older puppy. Older dogs are also good alternatives since you already know what they will look like as adults. Most of the time health problems have shown up, and temperaments can be evaluated.

Do not expect a small price tag simply because you don't want to show. Often the same qualities which make a dog a good show dog, or working dog, also make it a fine example of the breed, and a quality dog is a quality dog whether or not it ever steps into the show ring. Remember, breeders price their puppies by the quality of the puppy, not by the purpose of the buyer. However, some breeders may insist that certain puppies be shown as part of the buying contract. Be sure to inquire about show contracts if you are seeking top quality. Also, sales of bitch puppies sometimes include a demand for puppies back to the breeder as part of the purchase price. Think about this carefully. It will obligate you to working with the breeder for many years to come, and commits you to breeding a litter of puppies in the future when you may not want to do so.

If you are interested in showing or breeding the dog, you need to be honest about that up front. Don't try to get a show dog for a cheap price because you say it is for a pet. Today, AKC will allow breeders to mark papers as "non-breeding," which means that even though the dog or bitch may carry AKC papers, puppies from that animal may not be registered, even if bred to another AKC registered animal. You, as the new owner, cannot change the registration after the purchase. This has been done to try to reduce backyard breeding. Every year more breeders take this option for their pet puppies.

Ask the breeder about spaying and neutering contracts. Ask to see the contract. Most good breeders will have a contract for their puppies. Look carefully for clauses which may obligate you in ways you may not feel comfortable. Individual breeders may add conditions which affect your relationship with the breeder and your dog for years to come. One condition that many of our breeders require to some degree or other is that the puppy have early training. Especially if you are new to Rottweilers, it is worth the effort you will put into it. Recognize that your breeder understands your puppy and what the pup will need to know in order to grow into an adult dog which is a responsible member of society. Read the contract carefully and be sure you feel comfortable with it.

A good breeder will begin handling and socializing his puppies at a very early age and will be able to recognize the differences in their personalities.

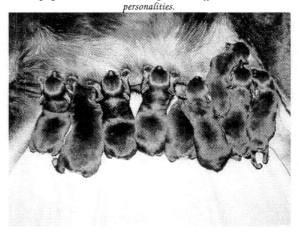

Ask what guarantee the breeder offers with the puppy. CAUTION: If you are seeking a show dog, don't expect a breeder to be able to pick out a group placing dog at eight weeks of age. These are few and far between, and a show dog is a product not only of his gene pool, but also of environmental factors in his up-bringing, how he is shown and conditioned, how he is presented in the ring, where he is shown, and what other dogs he is showing against on any given day. All a breeder can do is identify a quality prospect based on the pedigree and how the puppy looks in comparison to others from that bloodline. The more winners that have been produced in the past from the breeding, or from similar breedings, the better the chances of getting a winner, but don't expect the breeder to guarantee the success in the ring that often takes years to obtain. Remember, if you are looking for a show ring winner, find a pedigree where the parents, other litters, and other dogs in the pedigree have excelled in the ring. That may not guarantee that every puppy in the litter will be a winner, but it gives you a good chance. Better yet, find an older puppy or young adult that can be evaluated in the ring before you buy.

If you are interested in a working dog, one which will be able to successfully compete in Schutzhund or tracking for example, you will need to buy from a bloodline which has been successful in those areas to be sure your pup has the aptitude. But you will also need to put in the required time and training. Fine performances in these areas are not *born* into a dog, they are the result of taking a dog with aptitude as a working dog, and then carefully and consistently training him to bring out his talent.

Finally, if you are looking for a show dog, do not take your pup or young dog to the show and ask other breeders what they think of the animal you have purchased. Trust your breeder, or don't buy from him. Remember that dog showing is not only highly competitive, but it is subject to opinion. Many a good dog, in any breed, has gone back to the breeder because some new owner has taken it to a show, and listened to the opinion of other breeders — some of whom were motivated to say bad things about the entry simply because they did not want to compete against it! Your breeder knows the show game, his bloodlines and what a good dog should be. If he has shown for any number of years, he has a good feel for what will finish as a champion and what will not. *Many* of the dogs which are returned under those conditions *are* finished by the breeder.

Look at other adults in the kennel if you visit. This gives you an idea of what the breeder likes. How consistent the dogs are within his kennel will often tell you how successful he is at reproducing the kind of dog he likes. See if these dogs look and act like the kind of dog you are looking for. See the dam, and if possible the sire of the litter. These are all usually a good indication of the quality of the puppy.

A good breeder will want to know what kind of a home his pup will be going into. And he will be concerned that the individual pup will fit your family and your needs in a dog. In that way a good breeder is more like a social worker than a retail store supplying a product.

BUYING A DOG LONG DISTANCE

Sometimes it is necessary to buy a dog from a long distance. Don't panic. When you talk to the breeder on the phone, use the same technique you would use in person. Ask questions that will give you an idea about the experience of your breeder, how he or she feels about issues in the breed that are important to you and your family, how well he listens to what you want to use the dog for and how well he tries to match you with what is available. Find a breeder who enjoys his dogs, who knows what his bloodlines will produce, and who sounds like someone you can trust and have confidence in. Ask about guarantees, and expectations. This is the same thing you should be doing with a local breeder, or one whose kennel you visit to see a litter.

If you like what you hear, and feel that you will get a good puppy from this person, go ahead and buy the pup and have it shipped to you. Rottweiler pups ship well and will arrive safely, ready to adapt to their new home. Read the chapter on shipping and travel, but realize that it is better to get the dog which is right for you than it is to actually pick a puppy in a short visit to a local breeder. Although most of our breeders felt that shipping was safe and reasonable, some of our breeders were opposed to sending a puppy by plane. If you are looking for a puppy from some distance, be sure to ask the breeder how he feels about shipping.

WHAT NOT TO ASK A BREEDER

Don't ask a breeder what he thinks of another breeder by name. Ask for a reference if he has nothing available, or ask about the breeder's dogs. Ask the breeder how he sees the breed. But when you begin to ask about another breeder by name, you may get more information about the politics within the breed, and personal prejudices, both for and against, than real information about the quality of the dogs being bred by the other kennel. One breeder may like a certain type of dog and have nothing good to say about another breeder's dogs because they differ in style — without really giving the reason for the negative comment.

Remember also that dog breeding and showing are competitive. Over the years, disputes arise over wins and losses, or over personal issues that may have nothing to do with the quality of the dog or the purpose for which it was bred or what you want in a pup.

Do not expect to be able to come out to a breeder's home for a Sunday visit if you are simply looking at the breed for future reference. While some breeders have this kind of time, not all quality breeders do. Most of them show or compete in working events on the weekends, or they are dedicated hobby breeders who hold down other jobs and concentrate on their dogs rather than making dog sales. They will probably not have hours to spend on people who visit as something to do for the day.

Do not expect to handle a litter of puppies even if you are ready to buy. Many diseases are transmittable through handling and the breeder has no way of knowing what you have been exposed to. A breeder may ask you to only look at puppies. Breeders do not have the kind of inflated prices, nor the callous approach which allows them to simply write off the death of a puppy from overhandling, or being exposed to something a visitor may be carrying unknowingly.

Do not expect to view a litter shortly after birth. Most breeders will limit viewing to puppies which have been weaned. While it is a good idea to see the dam and the sire if possible, so that you have a good idea of what the puppy will grow up to look like, strangers around very young litters, (under five weeks) may irritate the bitch, and unless you are very familiar with the bloodline, you will probably not be able to see anything more than a cute lump.

And, if you have waited until the pups are ready to go home, don't expect to get first choice in pups. Many good breeders have reservations on their pups either before they are born or from shortly after the litter is whelped. Buyers who have placed their confidence in the breeder and his reputation have put a deposit on certain pups, which have been matched up with their new homes by the breeder. This does not mean that you will not get the "best" pup for you. Each pup and each new owner will be different. It is the breeder's job to match them as well as possible.

Rottweilers need a strong, stable and consistent home environment in order to develop to their full capacity as companion dogs who are kind with their family, yet protective.

WHAT A BREEDER MAY ASK OF YOU

Besides questions about your household, the breeder will want to know if you have any plans for training, exercise and socialization. He or she will make recommendations based on what he feels are the needs of the breed, and this pup in particular. He will ask you about other animals in your home, and what experience you have had with dogs in the past. They may ask you about your willingness to assume some financial obligations which owning a large dog will entail.

Breeders may ask that you have the puppy checked by your local veterinarian so that everyone can feel confident about the health of the puppy. (Do not expect most veterinarians to be experts on the finer points of conformation.)

WHAT A BREEDER SHOULD OFFER

Look for a breeder who is enthusiastic in talking about his dogs. A good breeder has put a lot of time and money into his breeding program. It is natural that he or she will talk freely and with knowledge about the pedigree, the individuals they own, and about the breed in general.

A breeder should offer a kennel pedigree of the dog. AKC will provide a certified copy of the actual pedigree for a fee, but breeders will usually give at least a handwritten copy with the puppy. This is not a certified pedigree, but it should be accurate based on

Rottweilers are very capable of doing a number of different jobs, but they need time and training to excel and become good members of society.

the breeder's kennel records. Champions should be marked.

A breeder should give you a record of the shots and worming for the puppy. Puppies should not leave a breeder without at least one set of shots, and most breeders automatically worm puppies. Puppies, like babies, put everything in their mouths and it is very easy for them to pick up parasites.

A breeder should offer instructions on what to feed the pup and how to care for it. Remember that no breeder is infallible. Even with the best of care and knowledgeable breeding, some puppy, sooner or later, will have a health or temperament problem. Breeders will usually not refund money, or assume vet bills, but many breeders will work with you to replace or exchange a puppy with a problem. Guarantees are usually less broad on an adult dog because health, temperament and conformation problems are easy to identify.

One legitimate reason many breeders do not give money back is because it would make the dog more an investment for the new owner than a member of the family. If breeders were to offer money back, they would be functioning as a savings bank, allowing the dog to be returned for the purchase price any time the new owners felt they no longer wanted the dog, or any time they needed the money. Most breeders prefer to feel that their dogs are going into homes where they will be appreciated and loved as members of the family. If the purpose of the buyer is truly to own a nice dog, then replacement is the logical solution, still giving the owner what he wanted in the first place — a loving, healthy pet. Another reason is that the best breeders are usually hobby breeders and often do not have the cash flow to refund the purchase price.

It is also necessary for you to remember that even though you are buying a puppy, it is more like adopting a member of the family than like buying a new car. This is not a business selling a product to a customer, but a reputable breeder, who cares about placing his or her puppy in an environment which will be good for both the puppy and the new family. A reputable breeder is more like a social worker than a profit and loss business person. He does not make his living breeding dogs, and he is not at a buyer's disposal in the same way that a business is at the disposal of its customers. But he will be concerned about you, finding the right dog for your family, and helping you to have a happy and rewarding life with your new dog. Please remember to treat a breeder accordingly.

A breeder may ask you to call and let him know how the puppy is getting along as it grows. Remember, sending a photo of the dog in his new home, and again as an adult, is a very nice thing that most of our breeders said they wished people would remember to do.

HEALTH

Hereditary problems are a fact of life with almost all dogs. Again, the reason to buy a pedigreed dog from a good breeder is that you have some idea what kind of health problems you may face, and how likely they are to show up in an individual animal. To think that there will be no health problems in any dog you buy, is like thinking you will raise a child without ever having to take him to the doctor. But by looking at which problems are found in the breed, knowing how frequently they occur and if you can cope with them as they arise, you will be prepared for what you may encounter before you buy a puppy.

Rottweilers follow the rule which says that the bigger the dog, the shorter the life span, the smaller the dog, the longer the life span. A Rottweiler will live to be ten to twelve years old, not bad for a dog of that size. Great Danes, for example, have a very short life span of only about seven years, so ten to twelve years for a dog the size of a Rottweiler is very good. Rottweilers move into old age very slowly, so the dog will be active throughout most of his life. As old age approaches, the Rottweiler will have a little stiffening of the joints, a little slowing of the gait, and a little graying around the muzzle.

Cancer is reported to be one of the major causes of death in old age for Rottweilers. We are seeing it more and more frequently in all breeds of dogs, though perhaps it is not so much that there is a higher rate of cancer in dogs now than there was twenty or thirty years ago, but simply that better diagnosis and more careful medical care allows dogs to live longer and to be more accurately diagnosed when cancer appears.

CANINE HIP DYSPLASIA (CHD)

Probably the most commonly *discussed* health problem in the breed is Canine Hip Dysplasia. The term covers a number of different deformities of the hip joint, which may or may not cause physical pain and crippling to the dog at some point is his life. The Orthopedic Foundation for Animals (OFA) keeps a registry for all breeds, and will evaluate X-rays of any dog over a year old, though a dog must be over two years old to receive an OFA Number. In some cases, OFA is a matter of controversy. Although many breeders swear by OFA, others criticize it for failing to collect data on parents, nutrition, previous health, environment and exercise during critical periods of a dog's life. Therefore, OFA has failed to compile the kind of meaningful data that might shed some further light on the problem. And although there are specific criteria for evaluating X-rays, there is a wide variety of X-ray equipment, technical skill, and cooperation of the dog, all of which affect the quality of the X-ray and the evaluation. Many dogs which are radiographically dysplastic, meaning that their hips will not pass the hip evaluation from a set of X-rays, will never be physiologically dysplastic, meaning that they will never show signs of pain or discomfort from this condition. Because of the size of the Rottweiler, however, physical discomfort such as lameness and pain are more common than in some of the smaller breeds. The type of dysplasia, the musculature and body build of the individual dog, and his life style and exercise requirements all have a lot to do with whether the dog will actually experience pain.

Whatever its shortcomings, many Rottweiler breeders have supported the efforts of OFA and have made a concerted attempt to improve the quality of the hips in their breed by breeding sound dogs to sound bitches. Many of the dogs in our Hall of Fame have listed their OFA numbers, and many more have OFA numbers which, for a variety of reasons, were not on the pedigrees which they submitted to our editors. It is only in recent years that AKC has begun to list OFA numbers and keep track of them, making them part of AKC records and public records of dogs. Therefore, dogs which were registered before that information was included do not carry their OFA number on the pedigree even though they may have such a number. Be sure to discuss this point with your breeder and see how he addresses the issue of Hip Dysplasia in the breed, what his feelings are on OFA, how clear his line is of hip problems, and how frequently his dogs turn up physiologically dysplastic. Also find out what their guarantee is if the dog is dysplastic and how they agree to measure dysplasia. A dog with Hip Dysplasia may well lead a long, happy and useful life, but it should not be bred.

LUXATING PATELLAS OR RUPTURED CRUCIATE LIGAMENT

A more commonly painful and crippling condition is luxating patellas, or an associated problem, ruptured cruciate ligament. The patella, or kneecap, is located only on the back leg, and should fit into a groove as it is held in place by the cruciate ligament. When the patella does not fit securely, it can pop out of the groove and cause temporary or more permanent lameness until it either pops back in or is put back through surgery or massage. The ligament may rupture and cause pain until it heals. Luxating patellas may show up as early as eight to ten weeks, so it is a good idea to ask the vet to check carefully when he does the original exam on your pup. A ruptured ligament may occur with movement, sudden twisting or loss of footing. In puppies, running through the house and slipping on slick floors, or worse yet, throw rugs which give way when the dog pushes off of them, may cause this painful condition. If this happens frequently, the ligament may stretch to the point where surgery is required. While both patella and ligament surgery are almost always successful (though costly), careful monitoring of the puppy will also help prevent the problem. There is some debate if these conditions are hereditary. Some lines do seem to have more problems than others with patellas and/or ligaments. But, since both problems are often a result of physical agility, energetic enthusiasm for life, and heavy structure, it may be that the dog's activity and attitude on life cause him to behave in a way more likely to encounter the problem than a dog from other, quieter lines.

EYE DISEASES

The Rottweiler does not have a high rate of cataracts, progressive retinal atrophy (PRA) or other eye diseases which are common in some breeds. Entropion however, is common. When the eyelid(s) roll inward, Entropion occurs. The degree to which they roll may vary, and sometimes it is very hard to diagnose if you do not know what you are looking for. Running or swollen eyes are one symptom. You will need to be aware of entropion and to watch for signs of it developing until after the dog is full-grown. It is important to remember that this is not a disease of the eye, but a condition of the eyelid, which, if left untreated, may lead to ulcers on the cornea and even blindness. Once the dog is fully grown, and the condition either has not occurred or has been corrected, it will not arise again. Entropion does not recur throughout the lifetime of the dog.

Ectropion is another common problem. A slack eyelid, usually the lower lid, causes the dog to have the look of a drunk. This is common for several breeds and does not cause any health problem or damage to the eye. It is strictly a cosmetic fault.

Ask your breeder about the frequency of these problems in his lines.

SKIN PROBLEMS

Many skin problems are caused by allergic reactions, but by far the most common cause of skin problems is fleas. For some reason, people often tend to deny that their dog has fleas, as if it is somehow a reflection on their home and care. In certain areas of the country, fleas are an ongoing battle, especially in the summer. Just because you don't see a flea doesn't mean that they aren't there. Regular spraying of the house, the yard and the dog will keep the problem under control. Once a dog gets a flea bite, especially if he is allergic to them, an infection may begin. Scratching with a dirty paw may lead to a bacterial infection, and the moisture from licking the area may lead to a fungus infection. At that point, any single treatment will not help because you are really dealing with several problems at the same time. The easiest thing to do is to keep the fleas from irritating the dog to begin with. If you see black specks on your dog, usually at the point of the shoulder, at the base of the tail or on the stomach or chest, he has a flea problem.

INBREEDING AND LINE BREEDING

Many people have come to blame health problems in modern breeds on line breeding and inbreeding. The problem is that many health problems are carried on recessive genes. It is possible that both parents may carry the gene for a certain health problem, but it does not show up in either one of them, because it is recessive. Yet, when they are bred together, the problem will show up in 25% of the puppies, because both parents carry the recessive gene.

When a breeder does a line breeding, all he is doing is doubling up on the gene pool. If the gene pool is strong, he keeps it from being invaded by recessive genes he does not want. If it is full of unwanted genes, which carry health, conformation or temperament problems, when he breeds close relatives he will have a higher percentage of pups with the problem because he is repeating the genetic pattern by breeding a stud to a bitch from the same gene pool. Thus line breeding — the breeding of a dog and a bitch with similar pedigrees and several relatives which are the same — may actually ensure that a problem will NOT occur if the breeding is done with a bloodline which does NOT carry the problem. Inbreeding, (the breeding of a sire to daughter, dam to son, full or half brother and sister - in short, two dogs which are VERY closely related), may produce a litter which is simply a repetition of what the breeder is trying to produce. The closer the breeding, the higher the likelihood that recessive traits will match up between sire and dam, and that puppies produced will exhibit these characteristics. Since recessive traits need to be carried on both sides in order to exhibit themselves in the puppy, the closer the breeding (repeating the same recessive traits over and over again), the more likely it is that any given recessive trait will exhibit itself in the puppies. The same is true, though to a lesser extent, for line breeding.

The difference between line breeding and inbreeding is only a matter of how closely the animals are related, and how often, over several generations, they are bred back to the same gene pool.

If a line is free of health problems, line breeding and inbreeding ensure that the puppies will be clear because there is no way for the recessive, offending gene to enter the gene pool. This is the argument breeders use for not outcrossing (introducing a new bloodline which may carry the unwanted recessive gene). But if the gene pool carries the of-

A working dog needs a different diet and different care than one which spends his time on the couch, just as a human athlete has different requirements than an office worker.

fending gene, line breeding and certainly inbreeding will increase the chances of it turning up. Because recessive genes are impossible to identify by looking at the dog, breeders often do test breedings of close relatives to see if the trait will show up. It is their way of finding out what is in their gene pool.

Although line breeding and inbreeding are part of the intricate study of genetics, and something breeders spend their lives learning about, it is sufficient to realize that the practice is no better and no worse than the quality of the stock from which the breeder started breeding. In itself, the practice does not mean that the puppies will be healthy, or unhealthy, crazy or calm, large or small. It simply means that whatever recessive genes are lurking under the surface, the tighter the breeding, the more likely they are to manifest themselves in puppies. Because of this function of line breeding, breeders who find a dog they like will often line breed to preserve the traits or "style" they like. It is their way of producing uniform dogs, that is, ones that all look alike in many ways when they are grown.

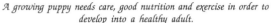

A growing puppy needs care, good nutrition and exercise in order to develop into a healthy adult.

PUPPY SHOTS

Your puppy will come to you with vaccinations. But be prepared that these days, with rapidly mutating virus strains, the pattern of vaccinations may be different than it was a number of years ago. Some breeders begin to vaccinate very early. Others use several different vaccine combinations and give them at different times. There are several new vaccines on the market, all claiming different properties.

Get a copy of the kind of shots and the dates the puppy received them, and take them to your vet. If your vet comments about the shots, remember that vaccination schedules are becoming more controversial every year, and that veterinary medicine is not an exact science. There are opinions and beliefs, and not all vets or breeders will agree. Our suggestion is to find a vet you feel comfortable with, and then fall into line with whatever he suggests. The fact is that puppies survive and prosper under a number of different programs; the important thing is to be sure that vaccinations are given.

Traditionally, puppies were given a combination vaccination at eight weeks, twelve weeks and sixteen weeks. Today, many breeders are beginning shots at five or six weeks. It is safe to say you should *never* take home a puppy that has not had at least the first in the series of vaccinations.

It is important to understand that vaccinations are not given in a set of three because it takes three doses to build up the immunity, but because of timing. All pups are born with maternal antibodies. This immunity, given by the mother to the puppy, will wear off sometime between eight and sixteen weeks, but there is no way to tell exactly when. If a shot is given while the mother's immunity is still effective, the puppy will simply throw off the vaccination rather than developing an immunity on his own. Thus, it is possible that a puppy which was given a vaccination at eight weeks, but whose maternal immunity did not wear off until twelve weeks, could be exposed to a virus at, say fifteen weeks, and would have no immunity at all. The mother's immunity prevented him from developing antibodies on his own when the original shot was given, but those maternal antibodies died off at twelve weeks, leaving him unprotected. The reason for the shots, which are traditionally given at eight, twelve and sixteen weeks is to ensure that a puppy is never left too long without either the dam's immunity, or the opportunity to develop antibodies on his own from a vaccination. Thus, no matter what shots a pup has received from his breeder, you will ALWAYS need to be sure he receives his final shot AFTER sixteen weeks of age in order to ensure that he has the antibodies he needs.

"Puppy shots," or combination shots, are DHLP+Parvo. That stands for Distemper, Hepatitis, Leptospirosis and Parainfluenza. Some breeders also give Bordatella and/or Corona vaccines, and some no longer give Leptospirosis.

Rabies vaccinations work much the same way, except that only the mature shot is given. Some states and vets require that shot to be given at four months of age. Others are of the opinion that four months is too young, and prefer to give the rabies vaccination after six months of age. Although DHLP and other vaccinations may be given by breeders, every state except Texas requires that rabies vaccinations be given by a veterinarian.

All dogs should be vaccinated again at one year of age and every year after that for the rest of their lives. Rabies shots should be given according to state laws, which vary in length of time a rabies vaccination will be considered "good."

Most of our breeders recommended that you do not expose the puppy to any other dogs until after the final puppy shot at four months of age. This means that he should not visit friends and relatives with dogs, he should not go to public parks and walkways, or any other area with heavy dog traffic. Even after inoculation, the titer (immunity in the blood) does not reach safe levels for approximately ten days after the vaccination.

Ask you local vet about heartworm, Lyme Disease, and a worming program which is right for your area. Climates, weather conditions and geographic locations make these vary from one state to another, and even from one area of the state to another. If you are buying a puppy from a warm, humid climate, the chances are that he may have worms. This is not a reflection on the breeder. Even with a conscientious worming program, breeders in the Southeast may have more problems with parasites than those in the hot, dry areas or the cold northern states.

SELECTING A VET

One of the most important decisions you will have to make is selecting a vet. Like doctors, not all vets are alike in their attitudes and treatment programs. Don't be alarmed if your breeder does not accept everything your vet may say about a puppy. Veterinarians have training in the health care of animals. They may have practiced for years in small animals or even specialize in dogs. But the breeder sees that particular bloodline, both the good and the bad, the healthy and the less perfect specimen over generations and over years. He often knows that particular animal far better than any vet who is seeing it for the first time and is judging by unrelated individuals or even unrelated breeds. There is some knowledge which comes with working with the same genetic pool for many years.

Although many vets are careful professionals, breeders have some recommendations in selecting a vet: First, ask your vet how he feels about a Rottweiler. Many of them are prejudiced against the breed. They may have dealt with an individual with a poor temperament, or the owner may not have been responsible enough to be sure the dog is well mannered in a strange situation. Rottweilers generally do not like being handled by strangers. Add to this that they are often either not feeling well when they see the vet, or they will be poked, prodded, and pricked at a routine checkup, and it is easy to see why many Rottweil-

ers take a dim view of the veterinarian's office and the humans who inhabit it. In defense of the veterinarian, he makes his living with his hands, and cannot be blamed for not wanting to get bitten. But if a vet approaches a Rottweiler with the idea that he may be in danger, he almost certainly will be! Rottweilers are bright and sensitive to humans. As an owner, it is your responsibility to have the training and control over your dog so as not to put your vet in danger. But it is also important that you talk to him before you bring your Rottweiler to him (even if he has treated another pet for you), to be sure that his attitude will not cause any problems. If he is not comfortable treating the dog, the dog will not be comfortable with him. It is best to investigate further and locate another vet who is more supportive of the breed.

Second, if your vet begins to make sweeping generalizations about the breed and your dog — especially on the first visit — think twice about what he is saying. Vets are not experts in specific breeds. They usually have only a working knowledge of breeds according to the dogs of that breed they have seen in their practice. Vets see unhealthy dogs more frequently than they see healthy ones. A healthy dog only comes in once a year for his regular inoculations, while an unhealthy specimen may be in the office all the time. Therefore, they may begin to base their opinion of the breed on the limited number of dogs they see on a regular basis without realizing that there may be many more specimens that they seldom see because they are perfectly healthy. If your vet begins to recite the health problems your pup will probably develop, especially if you have discussed these issues with your breeder and feel comfortable, don't argue, simply find another vet.

Finally, if your vet has recommended costly or unusual treatments — *get a second opinion.* This is simply good medical practice for humans or for dogs. And don't get the second opinion from another vet in the same office. People who work together often take the same approach to a problem. This makes for good working conditions, but it does not give a true second opinion.

HOLISTIC MEDICINE AS AN ALTERNATIVE

Recently, people have become very interested in natural healing alternatives commonly referred to as "holistic," "complementary" or "alternative" medicines. Acupuncture, chiropractic, nutrition, herbs and homeopathy are the most widespread alternative therapies available. This interest is expanding rapidly into the world of pets. Conventional medicine follows a reductionist philosophy, focusing on what is considered the exact location or cause of disease and attempting to kill it, remove it, or suppress it. For example, antibiotics are used to kill germs, tumors are removed or destroyed and allergic reactions are suppressed with drugs.

Practitioners of holistic or alternative medicines feel the problem is that none of these therapies address the real reasons the pet is sick. Healthy animals do not get serious infections, tumors or allergies. A pet's immune system is malfunctioning BEFORE these "diseases" occur. Therefore, what needs to be addressed is the functioning of the ENTIRE body, mind and spirit of the pet. Through this approach, the whole body functions better and it can prevent or cure almost anything, according to those who practice holistic medicine.

A wide variety of holistic remedies have been used on Rottweilers to varying degrees of success. There are a number of breeders and owners who believe the health of their pets has been improved with such practices.

Vaccination has become a focus for some practitioners of holistic medicine. Noting that some Rottweilers puppies develop the diseases for which they have recently been inoculated, some believe that elimination of such vaccinations is an alternative. Other breeders prefer to space out their vaccinations, or not to give them in combinations. Some breeders believe that annual boosters are not necessary, especially for dogs with other medi-

cal problems. The serious followers of holistic medicine feel that good nutrition and homeopathy can prevent these conditions as well if not better than vaccinations. **IT IS IMPORTANT TO NOTE THAT SIMPLY FOREGOING VACCINATIONS IS NOT THE ANSWER.** *If you are interested in holistic medicine, take the time to learn more about it and tailor it to your dog, his needs, and your ability to provide the necessary program.* Holistic medicine as a prevention of disease is based on maintaining good health through a number of different applications, *all* of which must be carefully maintained in order for the program to work!

Nutrition - The wide variety of opinions on dog nutrition has often led to conflicting nutritional programs. Food preservatives have been blamed by some for some allergic reactions. Others feel that pets suffer as a direct result of inadequate and even toxic pet foods. Still others feel that food must be fed as it is in nature — RAW and including organs and glands, bones, vegetables, live digestive bacteria and active enzymes. Almost all of these schools of thought hold that natural nutrition can improve virtually any condition and by itself cure a great many. Additives, such as those mentioned in our Shopping Arcade section, have been found by some breeders to improve the quality of life, from improving temperament and energy levels to eliminating skin or immune problems. Allergic dermatitis of all sorts, especially prevalent in Rottweilers, has often been traced to foods. Other problems found in Rottweilers which have responded to diet include kidney problems and disorders of the digestive tract, including colon problems and malabsorption.

Acupuncture - Acupuncture has been used for thousands of years. Its adherents believe that the life energy of the body (chi) flows through a series of channels (meridians). This energy is responsible for maintaining health and body functions. The energy may become excessive, deficient or blocked. There are points along the meridians through which the energy flow can be adjusted. This is usually accomplished through the use of needles. Lasers and pressure (acupressure) may also be used. Balancing and restoring energy flow can result in tremendous health benefits. With the improved health, diseases are eliminated.

A healthy dog has a shining coat and a happy, glowing look about him.

Chiropractic - The central nervous system is a major communications system within the body. Interference with nerve function can result in a tremendous number of symptoms. Physical and emotional stresses cause misalignment of spinal bones and impeded nerve communication. Chiropractic adjustments restore proper nervous system function, resulting in the elimination of a variety of health problems. There is another benefit to chiropractic that is not often discussed. Three acupuncture meridians (see above) run along and beside the spinal bones. Therefore, realigning the spine allows better energy flow.

Herbs - There are different systems of herbal medicine in use: Chinese, Western and Ayurvedic (from India). The Chinese and Ayurvedic approaches focus on the energy of the body. Different herbs are used to balance the body. The Chinese system attempts to balance Yin and Yang, the opposite types of energy within the body. If the body is too Yin, the herbalist balances it with Yang herbs and vice versa. There are also herbs to strengthen the life energy (chi) and cleanse and nourish the body. Western herbs focus more on the physical body. The herbs nourish and/or cleanse the body thereby strengthening its ability to heal.

Homeopathy - Homeopathy is a system of medicine which is nearly 200 years old. According to the law of similars, disease is cured by stimulating the body with an energy remedy. The remedy is derived from a substance which, if given in large doses, is capable of producing the same symptoms the patient is experiencing. For example, homeopathically prepared onion (allium cepa) may be given if a patient is experiencing tearing eyes, watery, irritating discharge from the nose and a desire for fresh air. Most of you would recognize these symptoms as those produced when exposed to the vapors of cut onions. However, these symptoms may also occur in someone with hayfever. The cause is not important. How the individual responds is what counts. This results in individualized remedy selection based on the patient, NOT THE DISEASE. The treatment of arthritis in ten dogs may require a different remedy for each one.

These are only a few of the holistic alternatives available. Others include massage, Bach flower essences, bio-magnets, scent and color therapy. The practitioners of all of these systems recognize the individual as a whole body with a mind and spirit, not as a liver or kidney problem. They realize that only the individual can heal him or herself. However, the healing mechanisms must be allowed to operate unhindered. Holistic healing methods maximize healing functions and remove existing impediments.

Rottweilers seem to do well with some of these treatments, though it is important to take the time to understand the process and to tailor it to your individual pet's needs.

Other varieties of holistic medicine include a balance between holistic and conventional medicine. First aid, basic health, nutritional balance, and basic remedies based on vitamins, minerals, trace elements and herbs are used to keep the dog healthy, improve his immune system and prevent common ailments before they develop.

BRINGING HOME A NEW DOG OR PUPPY

When you have selected your new dog, you need to prepare for its arrival. Decide who in the family is responsible for the care, feeding, exercise and discipline of the dog. Decide what rules the dog and the members of the family must live by. Rottweilers are very smart and will learn that different members of the family have different expectations. One member of the family may allow him on the bed, while another bedroom may be off limits entirely. Your dog will adapt to a routine. He may learn that one member must arrive home before he can go on his walk. He will learn where and how to go out to the bathroom, and when food will be provided. It is good to decide on a pattern of care before the dog or puppy arrives home.

If you have purchased an older dog, be prepared that although the dog may be housetrained in his old surroundings, it may take several days or even weeks to adjust to the pattern of the new family. Let him have time to adjust, but be firm in the rules. Limit his roaming of the house until he learns when and where to go out, and be firm but kind in correcting any accidents he may have. An older dog will take several weeks to feel at home in his new environment, but when he adjusts he will be ready to join right in with the new family, to travel and to meet friends and play with preteen or teenage children. Again, if you have children, be sure that the dog you purchase is used to children, and be sure the children are responsible in the way they handle the dog.

By contrast, a puppy is like any baby. He will need time to grow up, and he will take much more than a couple of weeks to be housebroken. More than likely he will go through a puppy stage where he will chew and carry things. He will take more time than an older dog. He will need training, care, attention, socialization and patience, as well as frequent feeding and sleep time that older dogs do not need.

Traveling with a puppy takes a little more time and energy. Don't feed or water him immediately before you leave. This will make it less likely that he will get car sick. Many pups get car sick and either throw up or drool constantly in a moving car, but most of them outgrow it by the time they are six or seven months old.

Puppies are fun. It is a great temptation for friends and family members to overpower a puppy, exhaust him, and even lower his resistance. Give the pup time to get adjusted to his new environment. Do not allow friends and family to carry him around to the point of exhaustion.

On the first night home, whether you have picked up the pup or had him flown in, be prepared that the pup will be lonely. It is likely that he has never been away from his littermates. He may be lonely when the lights go out. He may cry or carry on. A crate will be helpful as it will give him a sense of security (after he gets used to the confinement). Most of our breeders recommended using a #400 or #500 crate, which will give the pup plenty of space to move around, and will serve him as an adult dog for travel or sleep.

What to do with a pup when he begins to cry? Here our breeders were divided. Some thought the best thing was to let the pup get adjusted to being on his own. One breeder wrote, "Never take a crying pup out of a crate in the middle of his screaming — it will reinforce the crying and make the problem worse." Some thought that he should not be left alone, that he should be comforted. They suggested that the crate should be placed in the bedroom, or some area where the pup can be reached and taken out when he cries, given a pat or two and put back into the crate. One breeder suggested that the new owner sleep next to the crate to give the pup a secure feeling. We suggest you talk to your breeder and then evaluate your own personal philosophy. But remember that you will probably have to face the problem for a few nights at least and should decide ahead of time how you will handle it.

All breeders agree that it is VERY important to take the pup out to go to the bathroom first thing in the morning. When a pup wakes up, he will have to go to the bathroom immediately, and the faster you get him out, the less likely it is that he will have an accident in his crate. The more accidents he has in the crate, the more likely he will be to accept a dirty crate and the harder it will be to housetrain him. The ease of housetraining depends on the success in using the dog's own drive to be naturally clean if given a chance.

Let the pup investigate and have some time on his own. But don't ignore him. One of the best ways to housetrain him is to keep an eye on him, and stop him when he begins to have an accident.

When you bring your puppy home, you need to be prepared not only with bowls and beds but with a firm, consistent set of rules which will help him grow up into a happy, responsible adult.

Don't let him run the house. Every time he has an accident out of sight, he learns that using areas of the house that are out of sight is a good thing. Keep him in a small area and be alert. The more frequently you stop him in the act, and the more you keep him confined to a small area he wishes to keep clean, the more likely he is to train fast and well.

Get him into a routine. Remember, it takes six hours for food to go through a dog. Feed him and walk or let him out for exercise on a regular basis. This will help get his system used to the pattern of freedom and house living. Regular exercise in the form of walks or playtime will also help regulate his system. Be sure to monitor the pup outside too, and praise him every time he does his business in an area where you want him to do it.

Be sure the pup goes out first thing in the morning, and last thing at night. He may be in the crate eight to nine hours at night, and he needs to realize that the last trip outside, even if he has just been outside a few hours before, will be his last chance. He will get the idea soon, and will take the opportunity to use this last trip outside to empty as completely as possible.

Before you bring home any kind of dog or puppy, be prepared. Find out what the breeder is feeding and what the feeding schedule is. Get food and water bowls of appropriate size. Decide on a place for the dog to sleep, and be sure there is bedding for the dog. A blanket or bed may be good in the house, while shaving or straw in a box or a doghouse with bedding are useful for outside. If the dog is to spend time outside, be sure he has adequate shelter from sun and bad weather. Heat stroke is a leading cause of death in Rottweilers, so be sure the shelter he has is as cool as possible in the summer months.

Toys or chewbones are other things you may want to have on hand. Older dogs will need a leash and a collar, although a small pup will probably not be leash trained and may not be ready for it. Some of our breeders felt that a puppy should be leash trained immediately. Be careful to use a collar and lead which is appropriate for your pup, not a heavy choke collar that you would use on an adult dog. Start your pup with a soft adjustable collar such as a nylon choke or a small, thin choker which will not overpower him. Talk to your breeder about the best thing to use when training a pup to leash. Buckle-on collars tend to slip over the head, and choke collars should not be left on puppies because of the chance of accidental choking if the end of the collar is caught as the puppy plays.

Arrange to pick up your dog or pup at a time when you will be home. Fridays may be good, if you have time on the weekend to spend with him and help him get used to you as a new owner.

TRAINING A DOG YOU CAN LIVE WITH!

The key to successfully owning and enjoying a Rottweiler is good, sound, consistent training. Good training and exercise seem to be the hardest things for pet owners to understand and give their dogs. Rottweilers need much exercise, and they love to play. They feel best when they have some kind of useful pursuit for their time. They are extremely agile for their size and weight and can jump to catch a frisbee or scale an agility wall. We will talk more about all the things you can enjoy with your Rottweiler in the chapter on showing and competition. Take a good look at these endeavors and consider enriching your life and that of your dog with some of these skills and competitions.

Training and socialization, including exposure to a wide variety of people and environments, is a must. Some Rottweilers become reclusive with their owners, and if not exposed to the outside world early, exhibit fearful tendencies when taken into new situations. By temperament the Rottweiler should NOT be shy or fearful, but environment and experience play an important part in developing a good solid temperament which has been bred into the dog. Prepare yourself before the dog arrives to give him a good, well rounded upbringing so that you can enjoy years of companionship from a solid, loving pet.

Puppies tire easily. For the first few weeks, be sure he gets his sleep and is not exposed to the general dog population or places where dogs have been. Until they have had all of their shots and their immune system is mature, puppies may pick up infections that adult dogs do not. This mature immune system is usually in place by about six months of age. After he has matured, and adjusted to the new home, take him to family gatherings or walks in the neighborhood. Events such as ball games, outdoor programs, or time in the park are a good start. Take him with you in the car so that he gets used to traveling. Begin with small trips. Rottweilers can be good travelers if prepared from an early age to go with the family.

Puppies are cute and they often have behaviors which are cute for a puppy. For example, some of them will snap and bark if you stare at them. But each time you let this cute little puppy do something, ask yourself if this will be an acceptable behavior in a grown dog. If the answer is NO, don't let the puppy do it. When he gets used to a behavior, it is much harder to break his habits than to establish the ground rules to begin with.

THE BREEDER

A good breeder's job does not stop when the puppy goes home. Call the breeder when you arrive home, or when the dog arrives by plane, to let him know that everything is fine. Call him in a few weeks and discuss any problems or rewarding experiences you have had with your new family member. Remember, a breeder is interested in his puppies. Call to let the breeder know how the pup is fitting into the home; don't simply ignore the breeder unless there is a problem. Breeders are people too and like to get good news calls instead of just complaints. Send a photo whenever you can. It helps breeders evaluate their breeding programs and most of them truly enjoy hearing news of their "children."

Sometimes, due to changes in lifestyle or family pattern, it becomes necessary to find a new home for the dog. You should contact the breeder BEFORE you give the dog away to a new home or take him to the pound. They will usually either take the dog back, or help you find him a suitable home. Many breeders require this notice in their contracts, but we suggest that you make the effort to contact the breeder under such circumstances whether or not it is mentioned in your contract. Good breeders are interested in their dogs, and they wish to follow the life of the dog.

PAPERWORK

*T*he term "AKC registered" has meant, up until a few years ago, that a dog simply had a dam which carried AKC papers and a sire with AKC papers, both of the same breed. And in turn it could be bred to any other registered dog of the same breed, and the puppies could be registered. Any dog with two registered parents was eligible for registration and breeding regardless of its quality.

In recent years, AKC has responded to pressure to put some limit on the number of breeding dogs in the general population. Since 1991, dogs may be marked by their original breeder as "non-breedable." This designation means that the dog will be issued papers from the AKC with an orange, rather than a blue border. If such an animal is bred, even if bred to a dog or bitch with a regular blue bordered certificate with full breeding privileges, the puppies produced will not be eligible for registration.

When you buy a puppy, the breeder should give you two papers. The first, a blue registration application from AKC, and the second, a kennel pedigree. This will be on some kind of paper with a "tree" of names, like those in the "Hall of Fame" section. This lists the sire, dam, grandparents, and so on of the puppy. It will look something like this:

```
                                        grand sire of sire
                        sire of sire
                                        grand dam of sire
            sire
                                        grand sire of sire
                        dam of sire
                                        grand dam of sire
YOUR DOG
                                        grand sire of dam
                        sire of dam
                                        grand dam of dam
            dam
                                        grand sire of dam
                        dam of dam
                                        grand dam of dam
```

The registered name of a dog is often in two or three parts. The kennel name of the original breeder usually begins the name, followed by the name of the individual dog, and finally a second kennel name may follow if the dog was purchased as an unnamed puppy by another breeding kennel. This practice dates back to the early years in England when dogs were referred to by their owner's name first, because names in those days were very simple and duplication of names for dogs in the field was common. To make reference easier, people began to refer to the dogs as "Lord Grimstone's Susan," or the "Duke of Hamilton's Sam." These, combined with the year of their whelping, comprised the early pedigree records.

Today a dog may be named, as with the dog on page 79, "Ch. Big Country Boss of Oak Hill," nicknamed "Boss." The name shows that the dog named "Boss" was bred by Big Country Rottweilers (the Ch. before the name designates that he has earned his championship title), and was purchased as a puppy (before registration) by Don and Elizabeth Kressley of Oak Hill Rottweilers, who added their own kennel name at the end of the dog's registered name. Thus the dog is Ch. (the championship title earned through dog shows), Big Country (designating the breeder), Boss (the individual dog's name), of Oak Hill (owned by the Kressleys of Oak Hill Kennels).

Dogs bred and still owned by a breeder at the time of registration will carry only a kennel name, usually in front of the individual dog's name. On page 69 of our Hall of Fame, "Ch. Gamegards Femme Fatal" was bred by Victoria Weaver of Gamegards Rottweilers and the individual dog's name is Femme Fatal.

As explained on page 63, dogs who compete successfully earn titles which stay with them throughout their lives. Only conformation championship titles precede the name. Unless otherwise specified, "Ch." refers to an AKC title. Some dogs will have abbreviations of countries which indicate that they have earned conformation championships in more than one country. (Can/Am Ch. — would be Canadian, American Champion.) For example Am/Can/Ber Ch. Tri Z's Gringoe of Ironwood (page 68) is a champion in America, Canada and Bermuda.

Other titles follow the name of the dog. These include working titles, obedience titles and other levels of achievement, including the latest AKC title of recognition — CGC — Canine Good Citizen. Learn more about titles in the section on competition.

When you buy a puppy, it is possible that a breeder may not have the papers back from AKC, especially if the puppy is very young. But you should get some kind of kennel pedigree, and at least a note that assures you the puppy is registered.

If the breeder has the puppy registrations, they will be on blue paper. Be sure it is filled out completely. THIS IS NOT YOUR REGISTRATION CERTIFICATE. Ask your breeder about naming your puppy. Some breeders insist that pups are named with a certain letter of the alphabet to help them track their pups throughout the years. Sometimes this can lead to funny and awkward names, especially if the letter is "X", "Y" or "Q!" Other times they will require that a word or idea is included in the name. Look to see which box is checked at the top of the form with regard to breedability of the dog. Be sure the breeder has signed as owner of the litter. Finally, be sure that "sex" and "color" are checked on the front of the puppy registration form. Although it should be very obvious that a Rottweiler is

The BLUE litter registration will enable you to register your dog. Fill it out, including the name chosen for your dog, in the boxes provided. Fill in the color and the back of the form and send it to AKC for your dog's registration. THIS IS NOT YOUR REGISTRATION - AND YOU ONLY HAVE ONE YEAR FROM THE DATE THIS APPLICATION WAS ISSUED TO BE ABLE TO REGISTER YOUR DOG!

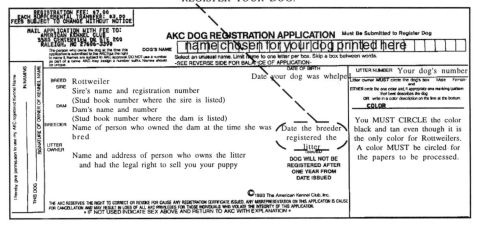

AMERICAN KENNEL CLUB

Name of your dog
NAME

Your dog's registration number
NUMBER

Rottweiler
BREED

Sex of your dog
SEX

Color of your dog
COLOR

Date your dog was whelped
DATE OF BIRTH

Sire's name and registration number
SIRE   (Stud book number where the sire is listed)

Dam's name and registration number
DAM   (Stud book number where the dam is listed)

Name of person who owned the dam at the time she
BREEDER   was bred

Date you registered your dog
CERTIFICATE ISSUED

IF A DATE APPEARS AFTER THE NAME AND
NUMBER OF THE SIRE AND DAM, IT INDICATES
THE ISSUE OF THE STUD BOOK REGISTER IN
WHICH THE SIRE OR DAM IS PUBLISHED.

Current owner of the dog - name and address
Your name and address will be listed here when
AKC sends you back the papers for your dog.

THIS CERTIFICATE ISSUED
WITH THE RIGHT TO COR-
RECT OR REVOKE BY THE
AMERICAN KENNEL CLUB

See Transfer Instructions
on Back of Certificate

REGISTRATION CERTIFICATE

The AKC registration certificate for your dog will be issued when you fill out your blue puppy registration and submit it to AKC with the required fee, or, if you have an older dog, when you transfer your dog's registration to your name.

black and tan, and that is the *only* choice you are given, if you fail to actually circle the color, the papers will be returned to you!

ACCORDING TO AKC RULES which have only been in effect a few years, YOU MUST REGISTER THE DOG WITHIN ONE YEAR OF THE TIME THE PUPPY PAPERS HAVE BEEN ISSUED, or it cannot be registered. Therefore, it is important to take

care of the paperwork as soon as possible.

Keep your kennel papers if you have them. If they were not provided, you can get a certified copy from AKC, or use a pedigree service such as the one mentioned in the Shopping Arcade Section. Canine Family Tree will provide you with a complete pedigree, usually faster, and less expensively than AKC. If you intend to breed your dog, you will most certainly need to know what is "behind" him or her. You will need to make inquiries about the strengths and weaknesses of these ancestors, and what will be most likely to match up with your pedigree to produce good quality puppies. If you intend to hire your male out for stud, bitch owners will ask to see a copy of the pedigree. If you wish to take your bitch to a stud for breeding, most stud owners will ask to see the pedigree before they agree to use their stud. They will want to look for lines with known health problems, and lines that will or will not match with those of their stud.

Even if you never intend to breed, it is worth the investment to send to a pedigree service such as Canine Family Tree and get a copy. Champions of record will be marked in red, and it is a chance to see what famous dogs are in your dog's pedigree. You may enjoy matching the pedigree with those listed in the "Hall of Fame" section, not only looking for particular individuals, but familiar kennel names.

AKC registrations are 8.5" X 4" with a blue border and the official AKC incorporation seal. It will also list the current owner and breeder. It also lists the name and number of the sire and dam and the small number in parenthesis after the registration number (i.e., 1-88) is the month and year of registration. It will NOT list the pedigree beyond the sire and dam of your dog. Send this information, and their registration numbers (or simply send a photocopy of the registration certificate) to the pedigree service for the complete pedigree.

If your dog is older and has already been registered, you will need to follow the "transfer instructions" on the back of the registration certificate. Fill out the back section A completely, be sure section B has been signed and send in the fee and the ORIGINAL CERTIFICATE. AKC will issue a new certificate, with you listed on the front as the owner.

If your AKC certificate comes back with an orange border, your dog has been marked "non-breedable" and puppies produced from him cannot be registered, even if bred to a pedigreed mate.

CARE

A Rottweiler requires very little special care. He is by nature a sound, healthy dog with few special grooming requirements. A good, well balanced diet, regular exercise, and clean living conditions with a warm, dry place to sleep will keep your Rottweiler healthy and happy for most of his life. An older dog may need slightly more care, a special diet for some, easier access to elevated doors, or a softer, warmer bed than he had when he was young, but for most of his life, the Rottweiler has few special requirements.

Diet is important. Ask your breeder about a good puppy food and try to maintain your pup on the same schedule and feeding program introduced by your breeder. Rottweiler pups are born rather small for the size they will eventually be when fully grown. Consequently, they grow very rapidly, actually doubling in weight each week during their early life. By eight weeks the pup will weigh around fifteen pounds, and will increase in weight at a rapid rate. For this reason, there is considerable strain and stress on immature bones and muscles. Most breeders advise that keeping a puppy in fat, cuddly, teddy bear condition can create orthopedic problems which may not be evident in the puppy, but which may only show up later in life.

A skinny and undernourished puppy is not necessary or even desirable, but you should keep your puppy lean. Puppies need good food, high in protein and fat to develop

properly, but they do not need to be excessively fat. Sometimes a puppy which is obviously well fed (fat!) will awake one morning looking like he has rickets! The front legs may bow out, and he may roll when he walks. Although the cause of this is under some debate, it is generally agreed that it primarily happens in puppies which are too heavy and on a diet too high in meat protein. Several of our breeders recommended cutting the puppy food with a low protein kibble for a few days and giving the pup plenty of exercise. (Sometimes this is hard to do because the pup looks like he is having a problem walking.) Trim off a little weight, and the legs will usually straighten out in a few days. Then, put him back onto a puppy food, though another brand or a slightly lower protein content might be wise until his bones have developed a little more. This condition generally occurs in pups between eight and eighteen weeks of age, and rarely happens after that time.

As we have indicated, exercise is of the utmost importance in raising a Rottweiler puppy. But you will need to be careful of the surface he runs upon. Slick vinyl floors, throw rugs which may give way underneath him, and beds or furniture that require him to jump on and off may be the cause of later problems. A puppy should have hard, rough surfaces to play on. Continuous living on soft carpet and grass will prevent the nails from wearing down and may spread the paws, leaving an unattractive foot. A puppy who gets lots of free play and exercise on a firm, rough surface will grow up with strong, sound bones and a good attitude. Some of our breeders recommend concrete, paving stones, hard dirt or gravel.

Since a puppy, and even an adult dog, spends a lot of time asleep, the bed is important. There are a wide variety of beds on the market which are very good. Outdoors, a blanket will get damp, and an ambitious, playful dog will pull it around, often creating several smaller beds from one larger one! Many breeders recommend the type which is suspended canvas or nylon on a PVC frame. These are easy to wash and keep clean, they keep the dog up off the damp ground, allowing air to circulate under the dog, and they are designed so that it is difficult for the dog to carry them around or destroy them.

Indoors these kinds of beds are also useful, or you may prefer some kind of large, soft bedding. But remember, whatever the type of bed, it must be easy to wash and keep clean. The problem with some of the large cushion beds is that by the time you buy one large enough for a full grown Rottweiler, there is not a washing machine made that will accommodate them! The kind with removable covers usually work well. Several of the companies featured in the Shopping Arcade carry these kinds of beds and other supplies such as bowls, collars and leashes.

Fencing is something else which will require attention. A full-sized Rottweiler has a powerful body and strong jaws. Lightweight fencing may be more expensive in the long run than a heavier gauge, more costly fence. A Rottweiler, left alone too long, will easily chew through the wire on the lightweight fence, and by the time it has been replaced or repaired several times, it would have been cheaper to invest in the more expensive type to begin with. Add to this the problem of the dog escaping when you are not home. Most of our breeders recommend good fencing as an absolute requirement for buying a Rottweiler.

As an owner, and good neighbor, you should be aware of the attitude of many people toward a Rottweiler. Although many Rotts have a wonderful temperament and are good neighbors, the publicity which has accompanied the breed over the last few decades makes it necessary for a Rottweiler owner to be responsible enough to be sure his dog is not out wandering the neighborhood and alarming the neighbors unnecessarily. For the same reason, our breeders strongly recommended good, sound training as part of the required responsibility of owning a Rottweiler.

The coat is reasonably short and requires little special attention. A bath from time to time will keep the dog clean, as some Rottweilers do have a distinctive odor. They do not take long to dry; a good toweling will get off most of the excess water. You may want to begin giving your Rottweiler regular baths early in life so that he gets used to them. Wrestling a full grown Rottweiler who is not used to a bath can be a real physical challenge! A blow dryer is a convenient way to dry the dog, and again, if you begin early, the dog will learn to tolerate, or even enjoy the experience. Be sure you keep the airflow warm but not hot and don't put the nozzle close enough to burn tender puppy skin.

Finally, many of our breeders recommend a vacuum for loose hair. Rotts do shed and a good brushing on a regular basis will keep the hair from flying all over the house. But if you begin early with a puppy, many owners find a vacuum a good way to get dirt and excess hair off the dog without making a mess or causing hair to fly all over. Although there are a few vacuums made especially for dogs, and several that are made for horses which will also work on dogs, you will find that the upholstery attachment of your home vacuums will probably do the trick. Many dogs develop a fondness for the vacuum that makes grooming easier and neater.

Ears should be checked and cleaned often. If the ear has an odor, is red or painful to the touch, or if the dog rubs his ears or shakes his head, or carries it cocked to one side, the ears are probably infected. A few drops of ear wash will help prevent infections. Fungus infections may be a problem in humid climates. If odor or other indications of infection appear, consult your vet for medication. Ear mites, may be another problem which requires treatment. Watch for odor in the ear area, or black "dirt" in the ear canal. If your dog has fleas, he probably also has ear mites. These conditions can easily be cured with a little time and low cost treatment. There are several good over-the-counter ear mite remedies which can be used if the black "dirt" appears.

Nails generally wear down with exercise on good solid ground, but if your dog lives in the house, on carpet, or on grass, they may need regular care. If you hear the nails clicking on the floor, or if they appear to be especially long, they should be cut back. Most of our breeders preferred to grind down nails rather than cut them. Rottweilers have black nails, which are difficult to cut back because it is impossible to see how far out the quick (or inner pulp) grows. When this is cut it will bleed, sometimes profusely. Grinding is a little slower and the grinder creates enough heat to cauterize the quick as it shortens the nail and prevents bleeding. Dogs usually respond better to grinding than cutting. Begin to grind your puppy's nails early and get him used to it and you will have less problem with his feet spreading out. And, by the time he is an adult, he will be used to the process and give you less trouble than if you wait until he is an adult before you try it for the first time.

DIET

Remember that feeding a dog is like feeding a baby. There are dozens of schools of thought and thousands of dollars spent by dog food companies to develop, research, and market their food. These high quality foods are complete and do not necessarily need to be supplemented with vitamins or other nutrients.

There are a number of excellent foods on the market. We suggest you talk to your breeder about what your dog has been used to eating. It is generally accepted that a puppy should be fed three to four times a day when he is very young, gradually decreasing the feedings to two by the time he is six months old, and an adult dog eats only once a day.

However, some of our breeders recommend free feeding, where the food is left in front of the dog all day and he feeds at will. Some days he may eat a lot, and some days he may eat almost nothing at all. Free fed dogs, contrary to popular belief, are not necessarily overweight, as they tend to pace themselves and eat at whatever pattern nature suggests. In good weight, you should not be able to feel the vertebrae along the backbone, but the dog should still have some definition in his body and loins. A puppy will eat almost as much as an adult dog.

Some dog foods have more bulk than others. Before you can say how much food a dog should eat a day, you must know if it is a high bulk or a low volume dog food. The obvious advantage to the low volume dog foods is that they produce less waste to clean up. High bulk dog foods are viewed by some breeders as being inferior because they contain filler. Others feel the bulk is good for the dog's digestive system. Following your breeder's recommendations, common sense and the food package instructions will provide guidelines for the quantity of food and timing of feeding for your dog at different stages of his life. Of course, in cold weather, a dog which is outside a great deal needs a higher fat and protein food to keep up his body weight.

Many of our breeders recommend dry dog food because it gives the puppy a chance to chew and strengthen his teeth. This chewing will help take the place of the shoes and corners of cabinets and save some of your sanity. Dry dog food also helps clean teeth, reducing the need for cleaning as the dog gets older.

Some breeders recommend adding 500 mg. of vitamin C per day to your dog's diet. They believe that vitamin C helps prevent hip dysplasia. Most breeders feel that a dog over two years has no further need for the added vitamins.

PARASITES

As we mentioned in an earlier chapter, the cause of many skin problems begins with fleas. Part of keeping the dog's environment clean is keeping it free of fleas. Many Rottweilers are allergic to fleas. Not only do they have a reaction to the bite, but scratching the area can lead to secondary infections. If you live in an area with a flea problem, be aware of it and treat it vigorously before it becomes a real problem.

Worming is another health maintenance issue. Puppies pick up things in their mouths, just as babies do, and the possibility of picking up worms is almost constant if they are anywhere another dog has been. Especially in southeastern climates where parasites are a problem, pups should be wormed by the breeder, and again with each shot. After that, worming should be done on a regular basis, depending on your area and climate conditions.

Heartworms are present across the country by now. There are a number of different types of medications for prevention. Treatment of an infected dog is costly and stressful on the dog. Prevention is much easier. When the dog goes in for his yearly health care and shots, he should be wormed and checked for heartworm. Ask your local vet what he recommends for treatment of heartworm in your area. Some of the heartworm medications available today include treatments which also eliminate other types of worms, such as round worms and whip worms, at the same time. These tablets are flavored and most dogs eat them as treats.

REGULAR SHOTS

Most Rottweilers seldom see the veterinarian. But yearly DHLP shots and Rabies shots according to your state regulations are also part of dog care. (See the chapter on health.)

DOG SHOWS
AND OTHER COMPETITIONS

*M*any a dog has lived his entire life as a companion, a friend and a confidant to his family without ever finding the need to have a career of his own. But some dogs do work for a living, and if they prove worthy, will earn a degree or title to attach to their names. The most common of these is a "Conformation" title from AKC. As you can see from our Hall of Fame section, dogs of outstanding quality and attitude are referred to as "Champion." (The title Ch. appears before their registered name, and is used every time the registered name is printed.) Once earned, this title, like all dog titles, will stay with the dog for the rest of his life. A champion is a champion for life.

Championships are earned by exhibiting at AKC sanctioned shows and collecting points. The number of points earned at each show will vary, depending on the number of dogs of that breed which are entered in competition and defeated. It takes fifteen points for a dog to be a champion, but at least twice in his life the dog must take a "Major," that is he must earn three points at one show. This is not as easy as it might seem since there are not many majors a year, and the dog must win the top award in heavy competition.

Points are awarded for each breed based on how many dogs are showing in the area each year. There are nine AKC divisions across the country and the points may be different for each division, and will be different for each sex and for each breed. The chart below lists a few examples of the way the points change between divisions. The Northeast includes Connecticut, Maine, Massachusetts, New Hampshire, New York, Rhode Island and Vermont. The Southeast includes Alabama, Arkansas, Florida, Georgia, Louisiana, Mississippi and South Carolina. The Midwest is Iowa, Kansas, Minnesota, Missouri, Nebraska and Wisconsin. The Southwest is Arizona, New Mexico, Oklahoma and Texas. There are three other divisions which are not listed below since the purpose of the chart is to give an idea of how points change, not an exact listing. The points refer to the number of points earned by the winner if a given number of dogs or bitches are showing.

Breeds with smaller numbers of dogs, or breeds with fewer dogs showing, will have very different numbers. Bloodhounds, for example, showing in the Northeast, would need

Location	Points	Dogs	Bitches	Location	Points	Dogs	Bitches
Northeast	1	4	5	Southwest	1	5	6
	2	10	13		2	14	16
	3	17	21		3	24	27
	4	22	27		4	30	33
	5	29	37		5	40	43
Southeast	1	4	5	California	1	6	7
	2	13	16		2	16	19
	3	23	28		3	26	32
	4	28	34		4	32	39
	5	37	46		5	43	52
Midwest	1	3	4	Alaska	1	2	2
	2	10	12		2	8	8
	3	18	21		3	14	15
	4	30	35		4	16	16
	5	52	59		5	19	19

only two dogs or bitches to earn a point, and four dogs or bitches showing would earn a major. This is because there are fewer Bloodhounds showing than there are Rottweilers. When fewer dogs show in any given year, AKC lowers the points needed for the next year. If more dogs show, the number of dogs or bitches needed for the same points will go up the following year. In this way AKC limits the number of champions in each breed to about 150 to 200 per year. A current, local listing of points for each breed can be found in the show catalog, or can be obtained through the AKC Event Records Office.

Rottweilers, for example, in 1996 in the Northeast, had to have only four dogs in competition to earn one point at a show, but it took five bitches in competition to earn a single point. It took ten dogs and thirteen bitches to bump that up to two points. To reach three points, a major, there had to be seventeen dogs or twenty-one bitches showing. A maximum of five points may be earned at any one show, but it would take twenty-nine dogs or thirty-seven bitches to reach that number. Even if there are a hundred dogs showing, only five points may be earned.

In the same year, in California, it took six dogs and seven bitches to earn a point, fourteen dogs and sixteen bitches to earn two points, and twenty-six dogs or thirty-two bitches to earn a major. Thus a dog or bitch showing in California would actually have to defeat a much larger number of other Rottweilers in order to finish his championship than a dog showing in Alaska. Points are determined by the location of the show, not the home of the dog. The new point system is printed each year in April and goes out with the AKC Calendar of Events, a monthly publication listing shows across the country for the next several months.

As you may have noticed from the point system, in the world of dog shows, a "dog" is a male and only a male, and a female is a "bitch." Classes in dog shows are divided by dogs and bitches. The top winning dog will be "Winners Dog," and the top winning female will be named "Winners Bitch." The best between them is the "Best of Winners."

In conformation competition, all entries for a class enter the ring at the same time. The judge looks at the entire class, standing, from the side and moving around the ring at the trot. The judge then "goes over" each entry, that is to say, he looks at the teeth and puts his hands on each dog to feel the structure. Each entry is then moved at the trot and the judge looks at the movement as the dog goes away, from the side, and as the dog returns to the judge. While in the ring, dogs are to stand at attention at all times and to behave with manners toward their handlers, the judge and other dogs.

To attend a show, call your local kennel club, watch the newspapers, look in the phone book which often lists yearly events in the area and will sometimes list the dog shows, call the AKC Event Records Office, or call your breeder. Once you are at a show, visit the vendors around the grounds. Those selling general merchandise will usually sell calendars with the shows listed on them. Some of our vendors in the Shopping Arcade also carry these calendars.

If you have never entered a dog in a show, perhaps the best thing to do is go and see what a show is like. Entries must be made two and a half weeks ahead of time, and a program is printed for each show, listing each dog entered, its name, owner, breeder and age. Dogs will show first. Puppy dogs, Novice dogs, Bred by Exhibitor dogs (those whose  breeders are actually showing them, American Bred dogs (open to any dog bred in the United States) and Open dog. The first place winners from each class will go back into the ring to pick Winners Dog. Then the bitches show, through the same classes, and the first place winners will return for Winners Bitch. Only the Winners Dog and Winners Bitch will win points — all other dogs and bitches will go home empty handed!!!

For that reason, people often hire handlers. These professionals know how to present a dog to its best advantage, and they know the judges and what certain judges are looking for in a dog. Sometimes owners will show their own dogs, and that is referred to as "owner handled." You may see that term in our Hall of Fame section. Sometimes a dog will even travel with the handler to the show and the owner does not attend at all. If your breeder sold you your dog with a contract which says he must be shown, you may be required to send the dog with a handler in order to get him "finished," that is, to earn his championship.

Once a dog has earned his title, he will show only in the "Best of Breed" class. Champions and the Winner's Dog and Winner's Bitch for the day will return to the ring to select the "Best of Breed." If the Best of Breed is a dog, a bitch will be chosen as "Best of Opposite Sex." If the Best of Breed is a bitch, a dog will be named Best of Opposite Sex. Only the Best of Breed will return to the group ring at the end of the day to compete in the "Group."

All breeds are divided into one of seven Groups: Sporting, Non-Sporting, Herding, Working, Terriers, Toys and Hounds. There are about fifteen to twenty breeds in each group. The winner of each group will return to the Best in Show ring where the final seven dogs compete to be named the "Best in the Show." You may have watched parts of the Group judging or Best in Show judging from Madison Square Garden on cable television. Other famous local shows are sometimes broadcast.

In the early days of showing, in the 1930's, all champions were in the Open Class and "Specials Only" meant your dog was for sale or on exhibition. Almost all shows were benched, with dogs tethered with chains. There were raised platforms in the middle of the ring which the judges used to compare exhibits, and the winner was always placed "On the Block." Most of the exhibitors were people of wealth and social position and owners seldom showed their own dogs.

Westminster was a three day affair offering benching. Colored cards in place of ribbons were displayed on the back of each dog's bench to help the public recognize the winners. Kennel men often spent the night on the benches with the dogs.

Today, the average AKC show will have about 1,000 to 1,500 dogs entered. Some will have entries of 2,500 to 3,500. One show in Louisville, Kentucky, has reached 5,000 entries! There is a lot of excitement at a show, and usually ten to twenty-five rings are being judged at once. If you do not have the judging schedule ahead of time and wish to be sure to see a certain breed, be sure to arrive about 8:30 in the morning. Some shows start as early as 8:00, and each breed is judged at a certain pre-scheduled time in a specific ring. A judging schedule is available ahead of time to exhibitors, and generally arrives in the mail about three to four days before the show. If you arrive too late, you may find that the breed you are interested in has already been judged early in the morning, and only the Best of Breed dog is still on the grounds. Or, the dogs may be back at their vans and cars, scattered across a large parking lot and almost impossible to find. We have very few classic Bench Shows left in

this country, so dogs are not on exhibit all day. They are brought up from their cars and vans, shown, and returned to rest until their owners are ready to go home.

HOW TO KNOW A STAR

Dog showing is a subjective sport. Participants like to talk and argue about the fine points of conformation. But almost everyone agrees that "Quality" and "Balance" are just as important as any single asset. Balance is reflected both in the way the front and rear of a dog go together, and in the way a dog moves. It refers to the proportions of the dog, and how it all fits together. But there is also another factor in a top winning dog. It is elusive, and cannot truly be defined, but it is called "presence." One breeder described a retired show dog at eight years of age: "He came into a large room, stood there and looked at you. Everything else in the room faded away. I have never seen a photograph that does him justice. The memory of him that day is implanted in my mind forever." A show dog with presence can sometimes have a few faults. He may not be as perfect as another dog, but he has a style, a quality, that like an actor or a model, sets him apart. He is charismatic, and a judge is attracted to him.

Some dogs are called "Package Dogs." They are nice in a number of ways. They may have a good head or topline, though not as good as some other entries. But they are good movers, have sound conformation, balance and presence. They have no large faults, so they go together in a well balanced package, and they are strong in a number of ways. This is what makes a truly great show dog.

But remember, there is no such thing as a perfect dog, or one which wins all the time. The top winning dog at Madison Square Garden, or at the National Specialty for the breed, may fail to get a ribbon the next day under a different judge. Opinions of judges will be different depending on their personal experiences and beliefs. The stronger the competition is between good dogs, the more disagreements there are between the winners because the finer points of judging require personal evaluation. There are no numerical standards. One characteristic may be listed as a fault, but so might another on a different dog and there is nothing to say which is better or which is worse. A judge may be looking at one dog with a good neck and head, but a bad tailset, while another has a wonderful topline, but a common head. These are values which must be subjectively weighed by a judge. What dog a judge ultimately points at (selects as his winner) depends on his personal beliefs of which is a

(continued on page 97)

HALL
OF
FAME

THE FOLLOWING SECTION IS A SHOWCASE FOR STARS OF THE BREED. All of the dogs pictured on the following pages are title holders. These animals will give you an idea how current outstanding individuals of the breed look and what bloodlines produce these qualities. The breeders and kennels listed on these pages represent a range of style within the breed. They have also been selected from across the country, giving you a chance to talk to a breeder in your area.

We congratulate the breeders and owners of these dogs for their dedication to fine Rottweilers. Their time and effort ensure the success of their dogs, and the continuation of the breed.

Here is an explanation of some of the titles you will see:

Ch. - champion — conformation titles precede the name. A listing of abbreviations of countries indicates that the dog is a champion of record in each of the countries outside the United States as listed. If no country is indicated, the dog is an AKC champion. (American Kennel Club)

Sieg - Sieger (means victory) There are five Sieger shows a year. The main winner in dogs is a Sieger and the main winner in bitches is a Siegrin.

Weltsg - World Sieger

WORKING TITLES

United Kennel Club working titles also precede the name. Most working titles will follow the name of the dog, as will titles of breed club recognition.

CD - companion dog, an obedience title.
CDX - companion dog excellent, the next level of obedience.
UD - utility dog, the highest level of obedience title. Abbreviations of countries before an obedience title indicates that the dog holds obedience titles in each of the countries listed.
Schutzhund is a sport that requires a dog to perform certain exercises in Tracking, Obedience and Protection. (See the chapter on shows and competitions.)
SchH I - First level of Schutzhund title
SchH II - Second level of Schutzhund title
SchH III - Third level of Schutzhund title
FH - Advanced Tracking title
IPO I, IPO II, IPO III - similar to Schutzhund titles.

BH - Temperament test with obedience. Must be passed before any SchH titles can be sought.
ZtP - Fit for breeding test. Requires temperament testing along with conformation evaluation. Dogs must be x-rayed clear of hip dysplasia to obtain the certificate for breeding.
ZtP V1A - "V-1" is the highest conformation rating and "A" is the highest temperament rating.
Angek - Hard core temperament test.
Korung - Temperament, conformation test.
TT - Temperament tested.
CGC - Canine Good Citizen, a title awarded by AKC through a specific test of obedience and temperament.
AD - Endurance test - American - Dog must go 12 miles in 2 1/2 hours and pass a temperament and obedience test.
VCX - Versatility Dog Excellent, Excels in many different categories, conformation, obedience and temperament.
ROM - Register of Merit - breed club designation indicating a dog which has produced the required number of titled puppies.
Bronze, Silver, Gold Sire/Dam - breed club designation indicating a dog which has produced the required number of titled puppies.

Please note that minor discrepancies in the presentation of titles are the result of breeder preference and lack of a universal protocol. You may see some additional titles we have not listed here. Ask your breeder about them.

FRONT COVER DOG:

Astor vom Landgraben, SchH III

ES/Intl. Ch. Ives Eulenspiegel, SchH III

Dina vom Kaiserberg

Berno von Remchingen, IPO III, AD, SchH III

Hektor vom Kleinen Born, SchH III

Issa vom Reichenbachle

Dixi vom Reichenbachle

FALKO VOM STEINKOPF, SchH III, AD, ZtP, TT, IPO III, WH, Korung

ES/Intl. Ch. Ives Eulenspiegel, SchH III

ES/BS/KS/Intl. Ch. Dingo vom Schwaiger Wappen, FH, SchH III

Anja vom Schwaiger Wappen, SchH I

Swenja vom Steinkopf, AD

Int. Ch. Benno vom Allgauer Tor, FH, SchH III

Esta Vom Steinkopf, FH, SchH I

Cora vom Leingarten

This German import, Falko Vom Steinkopf, earned his AD, ZtP, WH, TT, IPO III, SchH I, II & III and the prestigious Korung title. Falko competed past his 8th birthday in the demanding sport of Schutzhund always pronounced in courage. Falko has an "excellent" hip rating in both Germany and the United States. He is multi V-rated in conformation, winner of numerous Stud Dog Classes and is one of the most sought after studs in the United States. Falko exhibits and reproduces all of the traits most Rottweiler breeders try to achieve. Sound temperament and conformation with excellent working ability is predominate in his offspring. Now a retired working dog, Falko's awesome and charming character is full of the love to entertain and please his family by consistently showing off his greatness, Falko, pictured in his natural stance, exemplifies the dominate characteristics preferred in the breed of the Rottweiler.

Frank and Laura Alfano   **Alfalar Farms**
3308 W. Ohio Ave   **(813) 874-1273**
Tampa, FL 33607

REAR COVER DOG:

Abby represents "Nighthawk" Rottweilers in all respects. Abby is not only V-1 rated, she is also high scoring Schutzhund I with a score of 270. Abby was breeder/owner handled to all of her titles. In 1982, Daviann L. Brooks established Nighthawk Rottweilers. Daviann has been involved with dogs all her life, but her love for the Rottweiler came with the purchase of Michener's Michael CD, Certified Police Service dog ("Mick"). While Mick met all of her hopes and expectations, his hips unfortunately did not, and she was introduced to the harsh realities of breeding Rottweilers. Daviann neutered Mick and proceeded to purchase seven week old Ch. Einmin Lanneret V Rottdan, CD, AD, TDI, Police Service Dog, MRC Honor Roll. This dog, Hawk, later became the basis for her kennel name - Nighthawk Rottweilers.

Two years later, Daviann purchased her two foundation bitches, Ch. Pandemonium's Knockout and Can. Ch. Char-win's Cassandra, TT, from Valerie Cade of Pandemonium Rottweilers, a person she respects and admires greatly. With these two bitches and Hawk, Daviann went on to produce what eventually became one of the top producing conformation and working kennels on the West Coast.

To date, Nighthawk Rottweilers has bred seven litters and co-bred eight litters with enormous success. In conformation, Nighthawk has produced: fifteen champions and five pointed get, thirteen specialty winning get including ARC National Select, CRC Winners Bitch, GSRC Winners Bitch, ARC and CRC Best Brace and ARC National Best in Sweepstakes. Nighthawk is equally successful in the German Sieger Shows: six V-1 rated dogs plus five V rated, USRC National Most Beautiful Male, USRC National Youth Siegerin as well as five USRC Selects and four USRC Youth Sieger/Siegerins. Lastly, and equally important, Nighthawk has also produced several working dogs: two Schutzhund I, one Schutzhund II, two ZtPs, twenty obedience titles, one police bomb detection dog and seven herding instinct tested dogs.

Daviann L. Brooks
614 North Rodeo Drive   **Nighthawk Rottweilers**
Beverly Hills, CA   90210   **(310) 278-6645**

BIS & BISS AM/CAN CH. WINDROCK'S ROLEX

Ch. Rodsden's Zarras V Brabant, CD, Silver Sire
Ch. Birch Hill's Governor, CD, Gold Sire, MRC Hall of Fame
Ch. Rodsden's Birch Hill Bess, CD, TD, Silver Dam
Ch. Goldeiche Brick V Mikron, UD
Ch. Rodsden's Kane V Forstwald, CD, Gold Sire
Ch. Rodsden's Hella V Forstwald, TD
Ch. Rodsden's Roma V Brabant
BIS & BISS Am/Can Ch. Windrock's Rolex
Ch. Radio Ranch's Xtra Special, Bronze Sire
Ch. Winterhawk's Chief Justice, UDT, SchH I, MRC Hall of Fame
Ch. Winterhawk's Cobi V Bethel
Ch. Windrock's Fanni Von Richter
Ch. Donna J VT Yankee of Paulus, CDX, Gold Sire
Pinebrae Britta Ausdem Abend, CD
Irina Von Stolzenfels, CD

Rolex is the product of a well thought-out breeding program with a very strong pedigree both top and bottom. He finished his championship before age two while at the same time pursuing a career as an active therapy dog with his owner Bonnie Rosenberg. As a "Special," he has won the coveted Best In Show award as well as American Rottweiler Club Regional Specialty Best. In his three years being specialed he was always in the Top Ten. He is now living the "good life" playing with his boomer ball. He is more importantly proving his worth as a sire. He has produced Champions and obedience titled get. DOB 7/23/88, OFA # RO25450G25M. Breeder: Jane L. Justice.

Owner: Bonnie Rosenberg
11122 Alford
Brighton, MI 48116

Windrock
(810)632-6122
(313)485-8118

AM/CAN CH. HELKIRK WEISSENBURG'S CHANCE
OFA RO-29751

```
                                    Conner's Black Duke
                         Sunrise Seranade of Oakdale
                                    Rockin R's Robin
             Am/Can Ch. Mr. Impressive of Helkirk
                                    Celestial's Ample Delight
                         Gin Gin
                                    Heldegarde V. Circle T
Am/Can Ch. Helkirk Weissenburg's Chance
                                    Am/Can Ch. Rodsden's Zarras V Brabrant, Am/Can CD, Bronze Sire
                         Am/Can Ch. Birch Hill's Governor, Am/Can CD, Gold Sire
                                    Ch. Rodsden's Birch Hill's Bess, CD, Silver Dam
             Ch. Weissenburg's Fury
                                    Ch. Rodsden's Bruin V Hungerbuhl, CDX, Gold Sire
                         Am/Can Ch. Weissenburg's Don't-U-Dare, Gold Pt
                                    Ch. Marlee Bear V Gruenerwald, CD, Honor Roll
```

"Chance" is pictured winning Best of Opposite at the 1994 Colonial Rottweiler Club Specialty. Additional wins include the following: Best of Opposite 1994 Medallion Rottweiler Club, Best of Opposite 1994 Seminole Rottweiler Club of Greater Tallahassee, Award of Merit 1994 Kansas City Rottweiler Club Specialty, Best of Breed Levenworth Kennel Club with 214 Rottweiler entries, Best of Opposite 1992 ARC Regional VI Specialty and Award of Merit 1992 Medallion Rottweiler Club Specialty. She completed her championship in 6 shows with 4 majors.

Mike and Ann Stroud
Rt 1, 2704 Randy St
Amarillo, TX 79121
(806) 359-9355

Handled by
Perry Payson

AM/CAN CH. AMBERHAUS ERRIS VON ARA, CD

```
                          Igor vom Kastanienbaum, SchH III, FH
                  Ch. Eiko von Schwaiger Wappen, CDX, SchH III
                          Int. Ch. Anka vom Lohauserholtz, SchH III, FH
        Am/Can Ch. Goldeiche Ara von Brader, Am/Can CD, MRC Hall of Fame
                          Ch. Rodsden's Kane V Forstwald, TD, MRC Hall of Fame
                  Ch. Rodsden's Hella V Forstwald, TD, MRC Honor Roll
                          Ch. Rodsden's Roma V Brabant, MRC Hall of Fame
Am/Can Ch. Amberhaus Erris von Ara, CD, MRC Honor Roll
                          Int. Ch. Elko V Kastanienbaum, SchH I
                  Am/Can Ch. Rodsden's Elko Kastanienbaum, CDX, TD, Can CD, MRC HOF
                          Ch. Gundi V Reichenbachle, MRC Hall of Fame
        Ch. Twin Pine's Amber Again, CDX, MRC Hall of Fame
                          Ch. Rodsden's Bruin V Hungerbuhl, CDX, MRC Hall of Fame
                  Birch Hill's Marshall Heidi, CD
                          Am/Can Ch. Rodsden's Birch Hill Hanna, CDX, TD, MRC HOF
```

Am/Can Ch. Amberhaus Erris Von Ara, CD is a vital part of Blumehaus Rottweilers. Erris was owner-handled to his conformation and obedience titles. He has been used at stud on a very limited basis. With Erris as part of the foundation, Blumehaus puppies are exhibiting excellent type, temperament, movement, and soundness.

Merri Van Dyke
3315 Butternut Dr.
Holland, MI 49424

Blumehaus Rottweiler
(616) 399-1911

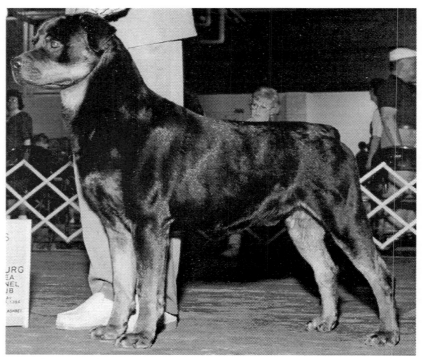

AM/CAN/BER CH. TRI Z'S GRINGOE OF IRONWOOD OFA EXCELLENT

```
                                    Ch. Rodsden's Elko Kastanienbaum, CDX, TD
                        Ch. Donnerschlag V Kertzenlicht, CDX, TD
                                    Phara Vom Haus Kertzenlicht, CD
            Ch. Ironwoods Gremlin
                                    Simba V H Brabantpark
                        Ch. Disco V H Brabantpark
                                    Quarta V Hagenbach
Am/Can/Ber Ch. Tri Z's Gringoe of Ironwood
                                    Ch. Rodsden's Ansel V Brabant
                        Ansel's Bing Von Brownlee
                                    Brownlee's Von Honey Bear
            Ch. CJ's Gertrude Vom Brownlee
                                    Tom's Jeff Davis
                        Burks Bruin Vom Lady
                                    Tom's Chasity Lady
```

Gringoe has a wonderful temperament and is a very devoted, loving companion and friend. He enjoys carrying firewood and amuses the grandchildren with rides by pulling them in a wagon or sled. As a show dog, Gringoe is a superb showman and representative of the breed with multiple credits to his name. Our dedication to Rottweilers allows us to plan selective breeding and produce the best.

Drs. John & Margaret Zazzaro
P.O. Box 990
Deep River, CT 06417

Tri Z Rottweilers
(860) 526-2655

CH. GAMEGARDS FEMMÉ FATÁL

```
                                    Int. Ch. Benno V Allgauertor, SchH III, FH, Bis
                          Int. Am/Can Ch. Bronco Vom Rauberfeld, Bis, SchH III, FH
                                    Centa V. Durschtal Gekort, Bis, SchH II
                 Srigo's Loaded For Bear
                                    Ch. Srigo's Zarras V Kurtz,  Silver Sire
                          Srigo's Of Thee I Sing
                                    Ch. Srigo's Elyssian Fields
   Ch. Gamegards Femme' Fatal
                                    Retsacnal  Autocrat
                          Rohirrm Seiglinde
                                    Gamegard's Lasting Light
                 Gamecards Black Britt (English Import)
                                    The Fuhrer From Gamegards
                          Gamegards Vitas
                                    Bhaluk Princess I'lenka
```

Femme is a well loved member of our family. In addition, she is widely recognized as an outstanding producer. When breeding, the biggest challange is to produce specimens that will, in turn, produce better than themselves. Even though Femme is an exemplary representative of the breed, many of her children are better than she. Some of her offspring include Ch. Gamegards Image De Femme, 1992 Best in Specialty, Award of Merit 1992 & 1994 Specialty Shows, Ch. Gamegards Moonraker, Best in Sweepstakes and Res. Winner's Dog 1993 Colonial Rottweiler Club Specialty. Additionally, several others are Specialty winners and champions.

Victoria F. Weaver   Gamegards Rottweilers
25260 Depue Landing   (410) 820-6093
Greensboro, MD 21639

V RATED MULTI-GROUP WINNER
CH. HANNERICH'S PARK AVE GENT, CD, CGC, TDI, OFA GOOD
CARDIAC # RO-CA18/76M/C-T

```
                        Am/Can Ch. Rodsden Elko Kastanienbaum, Am/Can CD,CDX, TD, Gold Sire
              Am/Can Birch Hill's Quincy, CD, TD, Gold Sire
                        Ch. Rodsdens Birch Hill Omega, CD, TD
        AKC/SKC/PR Ch. Vanlare's Ring Commander, HIC
                        Ch. Radio Ranch's Axel V Notara, Gold Sire
              Ch. Pomac's Lexa P. Vanlare, CD, HIC, Silver Dam
                        Ch. Hallmark's "The Sting", Silver Dam
Ch. Hannerich's Park Ave Gent, CD, CGC, TDI
                        Ulrich Von Der Brandt
              Sabian Von Wufgar
                        Burdett's Von Schalimar
        Me & My Shadow, CD, CGC, Producer of Merit
                        Am/Can Ch. Erich Von Paulus
              Deichmann's Deja
                        Pandemonium's Hana V Reimler
```

Medium large, correctly built male, very beautiful male head, large correctly set ears, slightly wet head (wrinkled), dark eyes, dark mouth pigment, very good topline, very good chest proportions, very good positioned front, slightly weak pasterns, correctly angulated rear, correct coat, dark brown markings, should be more defined on muzzle and chest, tight scissor bite, free far - reaching gait. V-2 Rated, Judge Dietrich Hufken.

Mike and Mary Donahue
226 NW 43rd St
Kansas City, MO 64116
(816) 454-4618

Handled by:
John Murphy & Tim Kernan

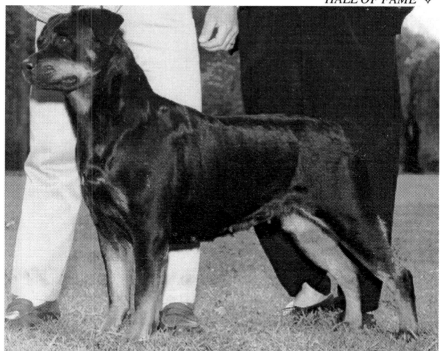

AM/CAN CH. MISTY LAKE'S DIAMOND CASCADE, CGC

```
                                    Am Ch. Freeger's Hektor
                          Am Ch. Lyndhausen's Arcturus Sunrise
                                    Am Ch. Shearwater Indian Sunrise
                 Am Ch. Cedar Knoll's Cowboy Joe
                                    Am Ch. Freeger's Nebuchadnezzar
                          Am Ch. Freeger's Samantha
                                    Am Ch. Frauke vom haus Schottroy
Am/Can Ch. Misty Lake's Diamond Cascade, CGC
                                    Am Ch. Graudstark's Luger, CD, TT
                          Am/Can Ch. Marksman Von Turick, CD
                                    Am Ch. Nobile's Shatten VonTurick
                 Am Ch. Diamond's Avatar
                                    Am Ch. Welkerhaus' Rommel, UD
                          Welkerhaus in Diamonds, Am, CDX, TD, UD
                                    Am Ch. Von Gallingen's Welkerhaus CIA, CD
```

Majorhausen's foundation was Can Ch. Northwind's Juno, CDX (HIT), SchH I, TT ("Tessa") — MRC/ Sovereign Halls of Fame/ARC Producer of Merit. In 1989 came "Cassie" another "dream come true"... Quebec Specialty WB, CRC Specialty First Am Bred/RWB; ARC Region I Specialty WB — finishing both Championships in six months! In three ADRK Sieger Shows, Cassie won V-2/V-3/V-4. Cassie's winning/ specialty-placing offspring: Am. Ch. Majorhausen's Hella Von Steinmetz, Can. Ch. Majorhausen's Jewel of Cade, V-1 Can Ch. Majorhausen's General Bull, CGC and V-2 Can Ch. Majorhausen's Go Midnight Blue, TT, BH (both sired by Tessa's son Am/Can Ch. Majorhausen's Elijah Blue, TT)... V-1 Majorhausen's Immortal Oliver (1994 Canada Youth Sieger)... V-Rated Am/Can Ch. Majorhausen's Heuer Boley (BPIS/ ARC Region I Specialty BW)...Am/Can Ch. Majorhausen's Haley of Hundehaus, CGC... Majorhausen's Von Fianna Ivy, Am CDX... Majorhausen's Immer Mein Schatz, Can CD. And now, our newest "stars on the horizon" are SG-2 Majorhausen's Jenna Cade, CGC and Majorhausen's Liberty Belle!

Patricia Major   Majorhausen Rottweilers
24 Cortina Street   CKC Registered 1979
Cantley, Quebec, Canada J8V 3B2   (819) 827-0365

SELECT CH. GAMEGARDS MOONRAKER
RO-42756E24M-T/RO-EL-999-T

```
                                    Ch. Donnerschlag V Kertzenlicht, CDX, TD
                          Ch. Ironwoods Code
                                    Ch. Disco Von Het Brabantpark
               Ch. Pioneers, D.J. Star Stuben, CD
                                    Select Am/Can Ch. Bronco Vom Rauberfeld, SchH III
                          Ch. Pioneers Das Bedazzled, CD
                                    Ch. Robil Marta von Donnaj
Select Ch. Gamegard's Moonraker
                                    Int/Am/Can Ch. Bronco Vom Rauberfeld, SchH III
                          Srigo's Loaded For Bear
                                    Srigos of Thee I Sing
               Ch. Gamegards Femme Fatal
                                    Rohirrim Sieglinde
                          Gamegards Black Britt
                                    Gamegards Vita
```

Select Ch. Gamegards Moonraker has had a brief but stellar show career. He was Best-In Sweeps at the 1993 Colonial Rottweiler Club Specialty defeating 236 other Rottweilers. Raker traveled to the 1993 Medallion Rottweiler Club Specialty where he was awarded Grand Prize Futurity Winner. He finished his championship in 1994 and was one of five select champion males at the American Rottweiler Club National Specialty Show, all of this before his second birthday! Winning ribbons is very nice, but Raker is at his best as a family dog. He loves our grandchildren and their friends. He happily plays with them for hours at a time. Raker guards our farm and home, easily discerning between strangers and familiar people. He is a real friend and true Rottweiler.

Ellen Walls and Henry Walls
Box 55
Hartly, DE 19953

Riegele Rottweilers
(302) 492-8615

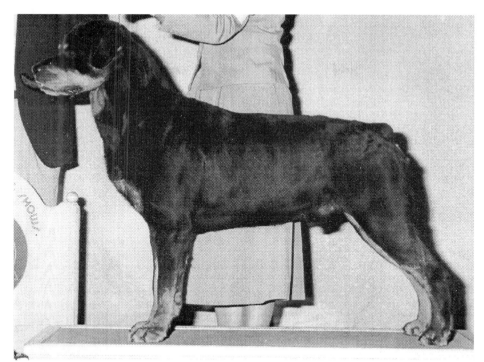

CH. CIMMERRONS BLUE KNIGHT, CD, TT, CGC, RTD

```
                                        Am/Can Ch. Rodsden's Elko V Kastanienbaum, CDX, TD,MRC HOF
                               Ch. Donnerschlag V Kertzenlicht, CDX, TD, Bronze Sire, MRC Hall of Fame
                                        Phara V H Kertzenlicht, CD
                    Ch. Ironwood Cade, Gold Sire
                                        Simba V H Babantpark
                               Ch. Disco V H Brabantpark, Silver Dam, MRC Hall of Fame
                                        Quarta V Hagenbach
     Ch. Cimmerrons Blue Knight, CD, TT, CGC, RTD
                                        Am/Can Ch. Trollegens Frodo, CD, Gold Sire
                               Ch. Van Tieleman's Cisco, CD, Bronze Sire
                                        Jameriss Gunda
                    Ch. Heidi V H Kertzenlicht, Am/Can CDX, UD, BH, RTD, Bronze Dam, MRC Honor Roll
                                        Ch. Rodsden's Axel V H Brabantpark, Gold Sire
                               Ch. Contessa V H Kertzenlicht, CD
                                        Ch. Rodsden's Frolich Burga, CD, TD, Bronze Dam
```

Lakeview Rottweilers is the home of Ch. Cimmerrons Blue Knight, CD, TT, RTD. Blue is a multiple Breed and Group Winner with wins at ARC, MRC, CRC, and KCRC Specialties. Blue is the number one sire of Specialty placing get in 1992 and 1993, including Winner's Bitch at KCRC Specialty and Best in Sweepstakes at the ARC National Specialty. Blue has sired multiple champions, Group Winners, and Top Ten get.

Tonya Renee Jones
390 Rottweiler Ln
Dawson Springs, KY 42408

Lakeview Rottweilers
(502) 797-5555

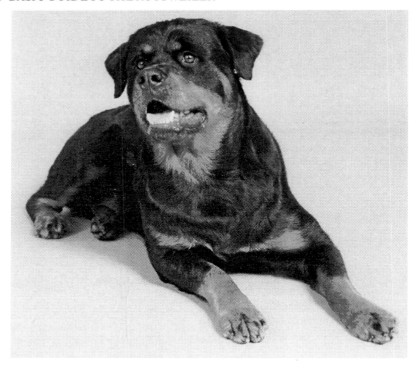

CH. VON WHELANS BELAIRE OF TOBANT, CD, CGC

Simba vh Brabantpark
Bis/Biss Ch. Nelson vh Brabantpark, MRC Hall of Fame, Gold Sire
Golda vh Barbantpark
Bis/Biss Ch. Tobants Grant
Ch. Rodsdens Autrey Kastanienbaum, CD
Tobants Texas Tootsie
Ch. Tobants Fancy Gal of LR
Ch. Von Whelans Belaire of Tobant, CD, CGC
BS Igor vom Kastanienbaum, SchH III, FH
Brando vom Dattelner Hof, SchH II, FH, IPO III, Gold Sire
Dolli vom Raesfelder Schloss, SchH III
AKC/SKC Ch. Tobants Honey Bun v Whelan, MRC Honor Roll
Ch. Gasto vom Liebersbacherhoff, CDX, TD, SchH I, Gold Sire
Tobants Sweet Sofie
Ch. Tobants Helka

Belaire received her Canine Good Citizen award at nine months of age. She completed her CD title at age 15 months. Belaire accomplished her championship owner-handled by the young age of 20 months. She has numerous Best of Breed wins over top ten males and females. Belaire was in the top ten throughout the year of 1993 All System at the age of 2 years! Her happy temperament, beautiful structure, and flowing movement makes her a breeder's dream come true.

Loretta and Allen Pyeatt
740 Alyssum Ave
Caswell Beach, NC 28465

Loral Rottweiler's
(910) 278-7762

CH. V-2 TBM CLEO LAINE, CD, CGC, TT, BBT
OFA # RO-35751G27F   CERF# RO-2207/94-48

```
                                    Int. Ch. Benno v Allgauer Tor, SchH III, FH
                        Xander vd Keizerslanden, SchH III, FH
                                    Noortje vd Keizerslanden
            Arinov's Boris Badinov
                                    Am/Can Ch. Graudstark's Pegasus, CD
                        Ch. Tulakes Echo, CD
                                    Ch. Tulakes Peach Creek
CH. V-2 TBM Cleo Laine, CD, CGC, TT, BBT
                                    Ch. Panamint First Nighter, CD
                        Talloaks Rowdy von Elz
                                    Desiree vd Klosterhardt
            V-2 Chloe Brandrew von Elz, CGC, TT
                                    Belico von White
                        Canon's Ursus Arctos
                                    Idyllwilds Roxi-Grotto
```

"Cleo" is Cubrienne's first Rottweiler. Bred by Tom & Barbara McCuen of TBM Rottweilers, she went on to prove she could do it all. At the tender age of one year and two days, Cleo won Winners Bitch and Best of Opposite Sex owner-handled by Adrienne. Expertly handled by Gladys Trout, Cleo finished her championship with 5 and 4 point majors. Cubby guided Cleo, the class clown, to her CD and BBT. Cleo has been owner-handled to multiple V ratings. Thanks to everyone whose love and patience have made this dream come true.

Owners: Cubrienne Rottweilers
Cubby Lash/Adrienne Perry
1905 Mountain View Ave
Flagstaff, AZ 86004
(520) 774-8088

Breeders: TBM Rottweilers
Tom/Barbara McCuen
6230 E. Peaks Pkwy
Flagstaff, AZ 86004
(520) 526-3816

AM/CAN CH. GEMSTONES BLITZ MEISTER, CD, CGC, TT

Eiko Vom Kastanienbaum
Ch. Rodsden's Elko Kastanienbaum, CDX, TD
Ch. Gundi Vom Reichenbachle
Ch. Rodsden's Berte v Zederwald, CDX
Ch. Rodsden's Querwind v Norsdwald
Ch. Rodsden's Yana v Nordwald
Ch. Rodsden's Sisu Vom Nordwald, CD
Ch. Gemstones Blitz Meister, CD
Ch. Igor Von Schauer
Ch. Northwind's Kaiser of Mallam
Ch. Northwind's Danka, CD
Eva Regnant of Gemstones, CD
Ch. Trollegens Bugler
Kipann's Heidi
Josephine Von Haus Dag

Blitz is a "Special" dog both in the show ring and the Riddle home. He has an impressive show record. He finished his Am. Ch. at the age of 14 months, owner-handled. Blitz has won multiple Best of Breeds and Group placements. With limited showing, he still ranked in the Top Ten Rottweilers in 1991 and Top Twenty Rottweilers in 1992. Blitz is a "born showman." His movement, conformation, temperament, and those dark, twinkling eyes have won the hearts and approval of many judges throughout the country for 9 years! Blitz earned his CD in the US and Canada in three consecutive trials. Blitz has produced multiple champions, spe-   cialty winning and obedience titled kids. Blitz is a joy to live with and a dream come true for us!   Von Riddle was established in 1982.

Karen & Harold Riddle Jr
156 Lovelace Dr
Fall Branch, TN 37656

Von Riddle Rottweilers
(615) 348-7479

AM/CAN CH. FRISIAN'S JAGER, CD

Igor Vom Kastanienbaum, SchH III, FH
Ch. Eiko Vom Schwaiger Wappen, CDX, SchH III, Gold Sire
Int Ch. Anka Vom Lohauserholtz, SchH III, FH
Bis, Biss Select Am/Can Ch. Goldeiche Ara Von Brader,Am/Can CD,MRC Hall of Fame,Gold Sire
Ch Rodsden's Kane V Forstwald, CD, Gold Sire, MRC Hall of Fame
Ch. Rodsden's Hella V Forstwald, TD, MRC Honor Roll
Ch. Rodsden's Roma V Brabant, MRC Hall of Fame
Am/Can Ch. Frisian's Jager, CD
Am/Can Ch. Rodsden's Zarras V Brabant,Am/Can CD,Silver Sire,MRC H/F
Am/ Can Ch. Birch Hill's Governor, Am/Can CD, TT, Gold Sire, MRC Hall of Fame
Ch. Rodsden's Birch Hill Bess, CD, TD, Silver Dam, MRC Hall of Fame
Countessa Von Beenen, CD
Can Ch. Fairvalley's Kluge
Ch. Anke Becker Von Beenen, CD, MRC Honor Roll
Bomark's Allison An Beenen, CD, TT, MRC Honor Roll

Am/Can Ch. Frisian's Jager, CD, began his show career at an early age. Bred by Don and Lin Beenen of Frisian Rottweilers in Lowell, Michigan, Jager was Winner's Dog at the 1992 Medallion Rottweiler Club Specialty from 12-18 month junior dog class. Following the rich heritage of winning Rottweilers in his pedigree, Jager continues to prove himself in the show ring. He has won several Best of Breeds and Group Placements in his young specials career. He is owned and loved by Dr. Royce and Marilyn Poel of Grand Rapids, Michigan.

Owners: Dr. Royce and Marilyn Poel
2690 Holtman Dr. NE
Grand Rapids, MI 49505
(616) 361-9290

Breeders: Don and Lin Beenen
Lowell, MI

CH. GOLDWINDS AMOR VON STEINTOR, CD, HIC, TT

Am/Can Ch. Rodsden's Elko Kastanienbaum, CDX, TD, Can CD
Am/Can Ch. Rodsden's Berte Von Zederwald, CDX
Ch. Rodsden's Yana V Nordwald, CD
Am/Can Ch. Cannon River Oil Tanker, TT, Am/Can CD
Ch. Radio Ranch's Axel Von Notara
Panda's Tugboat Annie
Ch. Gudron of Graudstark
Ch. Goldwinds Amor Von Steintor, CD, HIC, TT
Ch. Rangaar's A Sultan Rachmanov
Ch. Von Hawthorne's Max Otto-C
Von Hawthorne's Chiba F, CD
Am/Can Ch. Von Ravens Frolein Hannah, TT
Ch. Giaus Von Asgard
Sara Rose Von Asgard
Azure Von Schiker

Stonegate Manor is the home of Ch. Goldwinds Amor von Steintor, CD, HIC, TT. Amor is a multi Best of Breed and Group Placing son out of Am/Can Ch. Cannon River Oil Tanker, CD, TT. His far-reaching gait is how a Rottweiler should move. Amor produces puppies with beautiful heads, great movement, level toplines, great temperament, and bone. His children are winning in the breed and obedience rings. We are also home to Coldar's Liberty Bell, CD, HIC, TT who is competitive in the breed and obedience rings. Both Amor and Liberty are currently working on their Sch/TD Titles.

Bridget & Todd Intravartolo
2902 W. Gregg Dr
McHenry, IL 60050

Steintor Rottweilers
(815) 344-3607

CH. BIG COUNTRY BOSS OF OAK HILL

```
                            Igor Vom Kastanienbaum, SchH III
                 Brando Vom Dattlner Hof, SchH II
                            Doli Vom Raesfelder Schloss, SchH III
          Ch. Boss of Hale's Hollow
                            KS, BS, ES Int. Ch. Dingo V Schwaiger Wappen, SchH III
                 Bigi Vom Dorfbrunnen
                            Loni Von Der Grumannsheide
Ch. Big Country Boss of Oak Hill
                            Ch. Bethel Farms Apollo, Bronze Sire
                 Am/Can Ch. Luther Von Kruse
                            Ch. Olga Von Gruenerwald
          Big Country's Commotion
                            Int. Ch. Cacib Pio Vom Kastanienbaum, Bronze Sire
                 Am/Can Ch. Altars Mingen Magic V Amars
                            Ch. Gudrun Von Anderson, Bronze Dam
```

Boss finished his Championship before he was two years of age and is a multiple Best of Breed winner. He has an exceptional temperament, good bone, and good conformation. The best advice I can give anyone interested in a Rottweiler is to find a reputable breeder. We are fortunate to have gotten our start from a breeder as knowledgeable and caring as Johann Emedi. There has never been a time that he wasn't there for us when we needed him. Here at Oak Hill Rottweilers, we are dedicated to the betterment of our breed, for they are truly a noble dog.

Don & Elizabeth Kressley
Rt 2, Box 89 I
Delphi, IN 46923

Oak Hill Rottweilers
(317) 564-2485

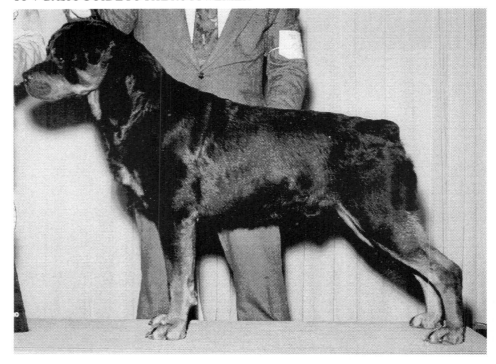

AM/CAN CH. MT FOREST DOMINIC OF RENNICK
AM/CAN CDX, AM UD

Kolja V Damerwald, SchH III, FH
Acht Vom Daemerwald
Malte V Damerwald, SchH I
Am/Can Ch. Saf Brutus of Pruhaus
Ch. Kiros V Lunsberg
Can Ch. Eltres Christel Aus Kiros
Monique's Kizzle Aus Drumer
Am/Can Ch. Mt Forest Dominic of Rennick, Am/Can CDX, Am UD
Am/Can Ch. Trollegens Frod, CD
Ch. Trollegens Benjamin
Ch. Nikkis Fair Lane Pictura
Von Russe's Atlantis Bryn
Am/Can Ch. Trollegens Frod, CD
Kamerade's Andromeda
Trollegens Josephine

Nico was only two years old when he completed his American Championship, shortly after followed his Canadian Championship. With limited showing he earned multiple Best of Breeds in both countries. Nico proved to be a strong working dog. Within his first year of obedience, he earned both his CD and CDX in a total of only eight shows. In 1993, Nico was ranked number one champion obedience dog. Nico was our first Conformation and Obedience dog. He was owner-handled to all of his titles and he is still working on more. Although these titles are excellent, Nico's greatest accomplishment is the wonderful companion he has been to all of us in the Rennick family. Rennick Rottweilers - Home of Champion Conformation and Obedience dogs. OFA RO-27173, RO-EL 681, Cerf RO 1366.

Don & Pat Rennick
P.O. Box 1904
Bothell, WA 98041

Rennick Rottweilers
(206) 742-6142

BISS AM/CAN CH. NORDIKE ALUGER LINDENWOOD, TT

Int. Ch. Elko Vom Kastaniembaum
Am/Can Ch. Rodsden's Elko Kastanienbaum, CDX, TD, Can CD, Gold Sire
Ch. Gundi Vom Reichenbachle, Silver Dam, MRC Honor Roll
Scharf Elko Von Regenbogen, TT, VB, Am/Can CDX, MRC Honor Roll
Rodsden's Gustav Du Trier
Tamaras Brandywine
Graudstark's Mariah
Biss Am/Can Ch. Nordike Aluger Lindenwood, TT
Benno Vom Amselhof, SchH III
Ch. Gasto Vom Liebersbacherhof, CDX, TD, SchH I, Gold Sire, MRC
Doli Vom Liebersbacherhof
Can Ch. Rodsden's Lindenwood Lamia, TT, VB, A/C CDX, MRC Hall of Fame, Bronze Dam, ARC Producer
Ch. Rodsden's Kane V Forstwald, CD, Gold Sire, MRC Hall of Fame
Ch. Rodsden's Heika V Forstwald, CD, VB, TT, Silver Dam, MRC Hall of Fame
Ch. Rodsden's Roma V Brabant, MRC Hall of Fame

'Luger's proudest moment in the ring coincided with his final appearance before retirement when he won the 1992 Medallion Rottweiler Club Specialty. Purchased as a pet from breeder Norma Dikeman, 'Luger exceeded expectations we did not even know we had! The thrill of his accomplishments in the show ring however, is matched by the personality and character of the dog we love who is truly part of our family. The ribbons, trophies,   and photos tell only part of who 'Luger is. The rest of the story is told day to day in his   gentle acceptance of all people and his goofy "Steal the Sock" game.

Tom & Laura Wurstner
2769 Lake Rd.
Silver Creek, NY 14136

Aluger Rottweilers
(716) 934-2430

QUINTA VOM OBERGROMBACHER SCHLOSS

Kai Von Tengen, SchH III, FH, GEKORT BIS EzA
Falko Vom Grutenblick, SchH III, FH, AD, IPO III, GEKORT BIS
Bea Von Der Hembachbrucke, SchH III, FH, AD
Klubsieger Norris Vom Grutenblick, SchH III, FH, AD, BH, IPO III, GEKORT BIS
Harras Vorm Sternbogen, SchH III, FH
Addi Vom Herrenholz, SchH III, FH, AD
Face Vom Grutenblick, SchH III, FH, AD, GEKORT BIS EzA
Quinta Vom Obergrombacher Schloss
Amigo Vom Kessback, SchH III
Hassan Vom Kongisgarten, SchH III, AD, GEKORT BIS
Gunda Vom Konisgarten, SchH I
Multi VI Iris Vom Obergrombacher Schloss, SchH II, AD, BH
Arras Von Der Herzogslinde, SchH III, FH, GEKORT BIS EzA
Berta Von Klien-Vach, SchH, AD
Vicki Vom Rodenstein, SchH I, FH

Heidelberg Kennels was founded in 1980. All breeding stock is either imported from Germany or bred from that stock. We have 12 indoor-outdoor runs that are heated in winter. We are experienced at breeding difficult bitches as well as doing artificial insemination. We have a small, but effective, in house labratory for breeding slides, etc. All Heidelburg puppies are guaranteed: AKC Registerable, to pass OFA at two years old, to be started with puppy immunizations, to be in good health at the time of purchase. The largest German Rottweiler kennel in the area.

Bob Gregory
W411 Highway 67
Lomira, WI 53048

Heidelberg Kennels
(414) 269-4478
fax (414) 269-4789

DINA V D TEUFELSBRUCKE, SchH I, BH, ZtPr

Int Ch. Dingo v Schaiger Wappen, SchH III, FH, GEK, EZA
Int Cc. Santo v Schwaiger Wappen, SchH III, FH, AD IPO III GEK
Int Ch. Itta v Zimmerplatz, SchH III, GEK
Benno vd Schwarzen Heide, SchH III, AD, IPO III
Bongo Von Noraksruh, SchH III, GEK, EZA
Lila v Hohenhamelin, SchH I, AD
Freya v Hohenhameln, SchH III, FH, GEK, EZA
Dina vd Teufelsbrucke, SchH I, BH, ZtPr
Kai v Tengen, SchH III, FH, GEK, EZA
Falko v Grutenblick, SchH III, FH, AD, GEK
Bea vd Hembachbrucke, SchH III, FH, AD, GEK, EZA
Bea vd Teufelsbrucke, SchH III, AD, GEK, EZA
Mingo v Hubertal, SchH III, AD, GEK, EZA
Int/VDH Golda v Sonnenberg, SchH I, FH, AD, GEK
Anja v Sonnenberg

Dina is the 1991 ARV National Club Youth Siegerin, the 1991 Landesgruppe Chicago Siegerin, and the 1991 ARV-USRC Regional Siegerin and Most Beautiful in Show. Her Grand-Dam was ADRK Klub Siegerin, her mother three times ADRK Bundesiegerin and ADRK Klub Youth Siegerin. Her litter brother Doc, was the IFR Siegerin. Her litter sister, Dorle, was ADRK Klub Siegerin. Her full sister, Face, was ADRK Klub Youth Siegerin. Her full brother, Falko, was IFR Sieger and ADRK Klub Sieger. Her sire, Benno, is the most titled Rottweiler in history and his sire, Santo, was a top producer in Germany and the U.S. Goldmoor is also the home of Ch. Itta v Salamandertal SchH I, AD, ZtPr and her daughter, Goldmoor's Lili, the 1991 East Regional Youth Siegerin. We strive to maintain excellence in conformation and the temperament intended for the true working Rottweiler. Breeders of show quality dogs since 1960.

Marge & Comann Gold
562 Goldmoor Dr.
Concord, NC 28025

Goldmoor
ROTTWEILERS

Goldmoor Rottweilers
(704) 782-2835

CH. FIDELIS' MANN OF PEACE, CDX

```
                                    Ch. Panamint Otso v Kraewel, UD
                        Ch. Elexi von der Gaarn
                                    Ch. Bimpse von Der Gaarn
            Ch. Rhomarks Axel v Lerchenfeld, UTD
                                    Lord Hannibal De Bratiana
                        Ch. Chelsea De Michaela, CD
                                    Astella Von Buell
Ch. Fidelis' Mann of Peace, CDX
                                    Walts Hofhund
                        Southwinds von Foxx
                                    Ruby's Alexia
            Ch. Tara of Fidelis, CD, TD
                                    Ch. Ivan Von Gruenerwald
                        Jody of Jesilieu
                                    Molzberg's Helva of Jesilieu
```

I would like to introduce a Legend Ch. Fidelis Mann of Peace, CDX, OFA EXC., Eye Cerf, Bronze Producer. Mann was just like the Good Dog Carl and more. He was also a Noble and Proud Show Dog. Mann's legend is living on at the Peixoto's Kennel. When you think of a Peixoto Rottweiler, you should think of a Noble, Square type, Loyal Friend and Protector to your home. Peixoto's encourage you to train your Rottweiler. Peixoto's offer puppies, stud service, obedience and conformation training and most of all a loyal companion. With every puppy you recieve free training, contract, guarantees. We are very dedicated to this breed. Buy from a Reputable Breeder! Proud breeders since 1982.

John or Kristy Peixoto
5309 Jenson Rd.
Castro Valley, CA 94546

Peixoto's Rottweilers
(510) 537-9193

CH. ANTREN'S DAILY DOUBLE, TT, CGC, TDI
OFA HIPS & EYES CERT.

Ch. Van Tieleman's Cisco, CD
Ch. Gatstuberget's Maximus, CD
Gatstuberget Giselle Gamine
Ch. Wisterias Bismark V Furhling, CDX
Ch. Elessar's Caius of Ebonstern
Ch. Gaerta's Wandering Wisteria
Panda's Tugboat Annie
Ch. Antren's Daily Double, TT, CGC, TDI
Ch. Bergsgardens Nero
Ch. Noblehaus Beretta
Ch. Noblehaus Ain't Misbehavin
Antren's All That Jazz, CD
Ch. Rodsdens Elko Kastanienbaum, CDX, TD
Ch. Doroh's Jaegerin V Noblehaus, CD
Ch. Doroh's Grand Escapade

"Smokey" finished his AKC championship by going Best of Breed three times and Best of Opposite in back to back weekends, defeating top specials. In his first show as a champion, he went Best of Breed at the Colonial Rottweiler Club supported entry to the Prestigious Philadelphia K.C. Show with an entry of 128. Smokey passed his temperament test and Canine Good Citizen test by the age of two. He is a practicing demonstration and therapy dog. In less than two years to date, Smokey has 25 Best of Breed titles, a Group 2, and two Group 4's. Smokey is owned and loved by Diane Romano with his breeders, Tony and Karen DiCicco, of Antren Rottweilers.

Anthony DiCicco
10 Oceanview Rd.
Lynbrook, NY 11563
(516) 593-6392

Diane Romano
(516) 887-5027

CH. DEXTER OF PHEASANT HILL FARM, SchH II, ZtP, CD, TT, OFA GOOD

```
                                    Ch. Brinker v Morgen Carroll
                         Ch. Rogers Summer Thunder
                                    Maja's Karitas Perpetua
              Ch. Ritmaur Aint No Mtn Hi Enuf
                                    Ch. Rogers Summer Thunder
                         Renruts Omen v Thunder, CD
                                    Golden Rules Heidi Lori
Ch. Dexter of Pheasant Hill Farm, SchH II, ZtP, CD, TT
                                    Gertase Kbuck
                         Deutscher Konig v Matlock
                                    Tiffanys Black Majesta
              Kaiserin Chelsi v Kuhnke
                                    Am/Can Ch. Erno vd Gaam, CD
                         Bergland Caper v Ein
                                    Lauffeuer Adrett Falco, CD
```

Dexter earned his working titles and was V-rated under nine different German judges in German-style shows in the U.S. He then competed in the AKC conformation ring, earning his Championship at age 5 1/2 and winning several Best of Breeds. He has offspring that are Schutzhund-titled, V-rated, and AKC-pointed. At Thunder Ranch Rottweilers, we believe that working ability is essential, and that it is proven only by working titles. Our goal is to build upon our German and Dutch bloodlines to produce a sound, healthy, intelligent, beautiful working dog.

Linda Gunderson
28802 Via Los Arboles
San Juan Capistrano, CA 92675

Thunder Ranch Rottweilers
(714) 493-2245

AM/CAN CH. EVRMOR'S QUIGLEY, CD

```
                                          Ch. Gasto Vom Liebersbacherhof, CDX, TD
                            Ch. Rodsden's Danzig V Gasto, CD, TD
                                          Ch. Rodsden's Toni V Forstwald, Am/Can CD
                Ch. Banta's Rowden Vom Danzig, CD
                                          Ch. Rodsden's Bruin V Hungerbuhl, CDX
                            Triple Oak Woodlands Calypso
                                          Ch. Woodland's Yankee Doo
Am/Can Ch. Evrmor's Quigley, CD
                                          Am/Can Ch. Van Tieleman's Cisco, CD
                            Am/Can Ch. Birch Hill's Ringmaster, UDTX
                                          Am/Can Ch. Birch Hill's Juno, CD, TD
                Drake's Dark Star
                                          Am/Can Ch. Rodsdens Berte V Zederwald, CDX
                            Gatstuberget's Oona of Evrmor, TT
                                          Ch. Gatstuberget's Hilma Honoris, CDX
```

Shown winning a Group I at Alberta KC in Canada. Family raised in the home, Quigley is one of many titleholders produced or living at Evrmor. In Rottweilers since 1974, I have strived for physically sound dogs with proper temperament. My dogs are out earning titles and being loved by the best puppy owners in the world. Evrmor bred or is home to twenty-three Canadian and American title holders including: Evrmor's Sweet Baby Jane, CDX, All Breed HIT; Evrmor's Lowenmark vd Berge, CDX, All Breed high scoring working dog; Am/Can Ch. Evrmor's Quigley, CD and Am/Can Ch. Evrmor's Que Osa Dulce, Am/Can CD, Specialty HIT.

Janna P. Morgan   Evrmor Kennels
2357 S. Lima St   (303) 745-0222
Aurora, CO 80014-1726

CH. VOM VIRAUS' JADED JASMINE
RO-46906G24F-T

```
                                Ch. Elko Vom Schwaiger Wappen, SchH III, CDX
                   Ch. Von Brader's Eiger
                                Am/Can Ch. Birch Hills Nanna V Brader, TD
        Bis/Biss Ch. Jade Hagen Kodiac, CDX, HIC
                                Ch. Gasto Vom Liebers Bacherhof, SchH II, CDX, TD
                   Liebs Kraus Von Baker, CD
                                Gretta Von Lieb, CD
Ch. Vom Viraus' Jaded Jasmine
                                Ch. Elko Vom Schwaiger Wappen, SchH III, CDX
                   Am/Can Ch. Trifecta's Barbarian V Murph, CD
                                Brandy Von Anderson, TT
        Ch. Vom Viraus' Sweet Jasmine, CGC
                                Kronprinz Karli Vom Alpen Haus
                   Ch. Vom Viraus' Black Shadow
                                Crystal Von Berberich, CD
```

Ch. Vom Viraus Jaded Jasmine is our 3rd generation of Champions. Jade, as she is called around the house, finished in style with two five-point majors (Breeder/Owner/Handled). We are glad that Jade has joined the Vom Viraus family of multi-champions, multi-specialty winners, group winners, best puppy dog, youth seiger, working/obedience titled, and great family companions. Jade finished her championship by seventeen months of age. We are basically private breeders, not a kennel, all dogs live in our home as part of our family. All puppies are raised in the same manner. We strongly believe that socializing and obedi- ence training go hand in hand in owning a Rottweiler.

Rich & Linda Berberich
P.O. Box 164
Dumont, NJ 07628

Vom Viraus Rottweilers
"Devoted Companions"
(201) 385-1626

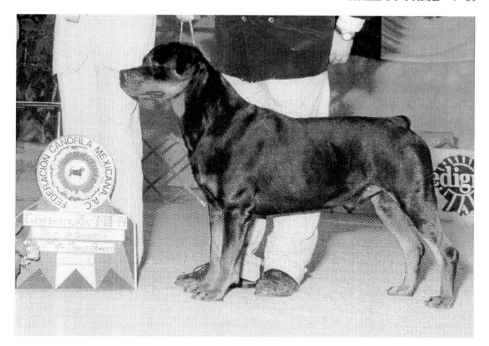

BIS, BISS CH. VON BAKER'S CARBON COPY, CD

                            Igor vom Kastanienbaum, SchH III, FH, ADRK, HD-Free
                  Ch. Eiko vom Schwaiger Wappen, SchH III, CDX
                        Int Ch. Anka vom Lohauserholz, SchH III, FH
        Ch. VonBrader's Eiger
                        A/C Ch. Rodsden's Elko vom Kastanienbaum, SchH I
                  A/C Ch. Birch Hill's Nanna v Brader, TD
                        Ch. Rodsden's Birch Hill Bess, CDTD
BIS/BISS Ch. Von Baker's Carbon Copy, CD
                        Benno vom Amselhof, SchH III, HD Free
                  Ch. Gasto vom Liebersbacherhof SchH I, CDX, TD, RO
                        Dolli vom Liebersbacherhof, HD-Free
        Liebs Kraus von Baker , CD
                        Hintz von Michelob
                  Gretta von Lieb Coletta, CD
                        Cubrina von Scott

Ditto, one of the "Fabulous Baker Boys," recently returned from Mexico with championships in seven countries, seven Best in Shows, a Best in Specialty Show, and the prestigious title "Champion of Los Americanas" (won under European Judges). He is now working on another obedience title while being specialed selectively in this country. Ditto's other accomplishments are as a pet and a stud dog. He is a companion to a family which includes children. His calm, affectionate temperament makes him easy to live with. Ditto's offspring have been winning in Central America and his first United States puppies are continuing the family's winning ways.

Patricia and Robert Baker
10288-68th Avenue
Allendale, Michigan 49401

Von Baker Rottweilers
(616) 895-6715
(616) 895-9623

UNO VOM KRESSBACH, BH
Imported from Germany

```
                                    Kai Von Tengen, HD, SchH III, FH
                    Falko Vom Gruntenblick, HD-Frei,  SchH III, FH, AD, IPO III,
                                    BIS Bea Von der Hembachbrucke, HD +/-,  SchH III, FH, AD,
          BIS Muck Vom Gruntenblick HD-Frei, SchH I, AD, IPO III
                                    BIS Ferres Vom Haus Winter, HD-Frei, SchH III
                    Duna Vom Gruntenblick, HD-Frei, SchH I, AD
                                    BIS Bea Von der Hembachbrucke, HD+/-, SchH III, FH, AD
    Uno Vom Kressbach, BH
                                    BIS Massan Vom Konigsgarten, HD-Frei, SchH III, AD
                    BIS Chris Vom Obergrombacher Schloss, HD Frei, SchH III, AD
                                    Berta Von Klein-Vach, HD-Frei, SchH II, AD
          Dina Vom Weissen Graben, HD-Frei, SchH I, BH
                                    Cliff Vom Waldhuck, Int/Vom-Ch., HD+/-, SchH III
                    Dixi Vom Eisplatz, HD-Frei, SchH I
                                    Xanti Vom Rodenstein, HD+, SchH I
```

Radio Ranch has been involved in showing and breeding Rottweilers for over 25 years. Our Ch. Radio Ranch's Axel von Notara was a top ten winner for three years and a Best of Breed Winner at Westminster. He is also a top producer of Champions. Radio Ranch has owned and bred many specialty winners and has imported some top winners from Europe to add to a small select breeding program. Our Ch. Radio Ranch's Axel V. Notare is featured on the cover of *The Book of the Rottweiler* by Anna Katherine Nichols. Our pups are family raised and placed in loving homes.

Pamela C. Brown and Carolyn Ferguson
1321 Barbara Ct.
Chesapeake, Va 23322

Radio Ranch
(804) 421-3072
(804) 246-8601

V-2 CH. BLAKE VON EBON-BEHR, TT, OFA EXCELLENT

```
                              Int Ch. Benno V Allgauer Tor, SchH III
                     Dux Vom Rauchfang, SchH III, FH
                              Burga V Rauchfang, SchH I
           Dux's Blitz Von Offenbach, OFA Excellent
                              Cliff V LuckShof, SchH II
                     Elke Vom Magdeberg, Sch II
                              Babbette vom Magdeberg, SchH  I
V-2 Ch. Blake Von Ebon-Behr, TT, OFA Excellent
                              Ch. Wotan vom Kastanienbaum
                     Ch. Wokan vom Sonnenhaus, CD, OFA Good
                              Ch. Greta Michaela
           Ms. Javlin vom Winthaus, CD, TT
                              Ch. Rocky von Anderson
                     Juliet vom Winthaus, CD, OFA Good
                              Dana M Von Goldenwest
```

Blake finished in the summer class of 1990 out of the Bred-By-Exhibitor class and received his first major at seventeen months. Blake finished with three majors and currently has several offspring nearing championship status. Ebon-Behr Kennel breeds for working, conformation, type, and temperament! Please keep in mind: Rottweilers are not for everyone. Please do the breed a favor and think carefully before buying a Rottweiler. They are a working breed who require a lot of time and good training. However, they are also very loving with excellent qualities. Please speak with different breeders and collect as much information as possible.

Gladys Trout
8615 Shasta Rd.
Phelan, CA 92371

Ebon-Behr Rottweilers
(619) 947- 7960

BIS/BISS/AM/CAN/BDA CH. PIONEER'S DJ STAR STUBEN A/BDA,CD,CGC,TDI

```
                                        Ch. Rodsden's Elko Kastanienbaum, CDX, TD, Can CD
                        Ch. Donnerschlag V. Kertzenlicht, CDX, TD
                                        Phara Vom Hause Kertzenlight, CD
        BIS Ch. Ironwood's Cade, CD, CGC
                                        Simba V.H. Brabantpark
                        Chh. Disco V.H. Brabantpark
                                        Ouarta V. Hagenbach
BIS/BISS/Am/Can/Bda Ch. Pioneer's DJ Star Stuben, CD, CGC, TDI
                                        Ch. Benno Vom Allgauer Tor, SchH III, FH
                        Ch. Bronco Vom Rauberfeld, SchH III, FH
                                        Centa Vom Durschtal, SchH III
        Ch. Pioneer's Das Bedazzled, CD
                                        Ch. Donnaj VT. Yankee of Paulus, CDX, TT
                        Ch. Robil Marta Von Donnaj
                                        Donnaj Touch of Class
```

Mr. Stubbs finished his championship by going Best in Specialty Show at the Colonial Rottweiler Club in 1991 from the open dog class. Since then he has gone on to recieve Canadian and Bermudian Championships, his American & Bermudian CD's, another BISS, a Best in Show, and finished #2 Rottweiler all breed in 1994. He now devotes time to being a therapy dog and carting. His childeren are carrying on the winning tradition with multiple wins in breed, group and BIS, as well as achieving distinction in tracking, odedience, herding, and carting. The philosophy at Sidecar Rottweiler is to produce dogs with stable temperaments who are outstanding all around companions!

Joan Eversole, DMD
2 South Main St.
Plymouth, NH 03264

Sidecar Rottweilers
(603) 536-1530

BIS SELECT CH. WINDROCK'S JACK HAMMER
OFA-RO-41212G24M   Cardiac #RO-4

```
                              Ch. Donnerschlag V. Kertzenlight
                    BIS Select Ch. Ironwood's Cade, CD, Gold Producer
                              Ch. Disco VH Brabantpark
          BIS/BISS Select A/C Ch. Pioneers DJ Star Stuben, CD
                                    KS INT/A/C Ch. Bronco Von Rauberfeld, SchH III, FH
                    Ch. Pioneer's Das Bedazzled
                              Ch. Robil Marta Von Donnaj
BIS Select Ch. Windrock's Jack Hammer
                                    BIS/BISS Select A/C Ch. Birch Hill's Governor, A/C CD
                    A/C Ch. Goldeiche Brick V. Mikon, UD
                              Ch. Rodsden's Hella V Forstwald, TD
          A/C Ch. Windrock's Sophie V. Richter
                                    Can. OTCH A/C Ch.  Winterhawk's Chief Justice, A/C UDT, SchHI
                    A/C Ch. Windrock's Fanni V Richter
                              Pinebrae's Britta Aus dem Abend, A/C CD
```

Best in Show, Select Ch. Windrock's Jack Hammer. "Hammer" is proudly pictured across from his father, Best in Show, BISS, Select A/C Ch. Pioneer's DJ Star Stuben CD. Hammer started following in his father's winning footsteps by winning a 5pt. major from the puppy class and went on to finish his AKC championship, owner-handled at 15 months of age. Hammer then joined his father in the 1994 Top Ten rankings, the first father and son team to both be ranked in the same year. Hammer is currently ranked as the #1 Rottweiler in the country.

Owned by: Matt & Lorene Jones
1125 Lafayette St.
Middletown, OH 45044
(513) 727-0179

Co-owned by: Joan Eversole, DMD
(603) 536-1530

LACKY V ARATORA, SchH II, GEKORT

"Thank You For Your Love And Devotion"
"Once Gone From This Earth, None Can Take Your Place, "
"You Were Unique"

```
                          Conny v.d. Albrechtsburg SchH III, FH  I
              Jalk v. Teufelsberg, SchH I
                          Conny v. Teufelsburg, SchH I
Lacky v Aratora, SchH II, GEKORT
                          Quant v. Winkel SchH III DDR- Sieger'82
              Gunda v. Aratora SchH I
                          Carmen v.d. Sachsenburg, SchH I
```

Frolic'n Kennels has always had the goal of owning, exhibiting, and producing the versatile Rottweiler. Our ideal Rottweiler is one who is able to compete in conformation and working all the while remaining a best friend. Lacky earned the titles 1987 DDR Puppy Sieger, 1988 DDR Youth Sieger, 1989 DDR Sieger. In addition to Lacky, Frolic'n Kennel has had the privilege of providing a loving home for outstanding Rottweilers who will never be forgotten in the history of the breed. Among those are Am/Can Ch. Panamint Nobel V Falkenberg, CD; Am/BDA, Can/Mex, CACIB Ch. Jack Vom Emstal, Am/Can CD, Mex PC, SchH I; Am/Can/Mex Ch. '78 World Siegerin Uschi Vom Hause Henseler, CD, SchH I; Am/Can/Mex Ch. Panamint Rani v d Sandhaufen CD; Ch. Arras Vom Schloss Stutensee, CDX, TD, SchH III, IPO III, FH, AD, Gekort BIS EzA; Ch. Frolic'n Darth Vader, CDX; Hanni v d Bergschmiede SchH III, IPO III, FH; Ch. Endikai Von Edelhart CD, B, SchH I. These dogs were group placing and/or were Producers of Merit despite limited showing and breeding. There have been and still are other Rottweilers in our lives and hearts. They have also received titles and given love too extensive to measure.

Stephen and Charlotte
Wanda and Steve
116 - 214th. Ave SE
Redmond, WA 98053

Frolic'n Kennel
(206) 883-8186
(206) 869-5291

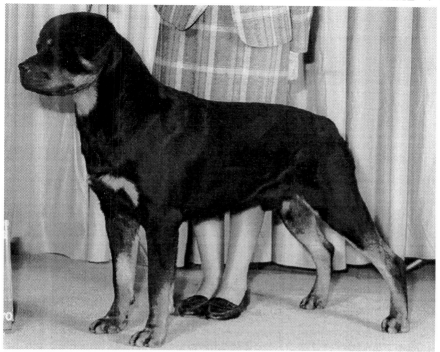

CH. FOXY'S GENESIS V WINDSTORM, CGC, TDI
OFA Hips RO-39716 Good/ OFA Elbows EL-714

Am/Can Ch. Trifecta's Barbarian v Murph, CD

Ch. Von Hottensteins I Marc

Ch. Von Hottenstein's A Dare

Am/Can Ch. Foxy's Follow That Dream, CGC, TDI

Zum Verkauf's Eric Behalter

Ch. Fraulein Gretchen von Fox, CD, TT, CGC

Demon von Fox, CD

Ch. Foxy's Genesis V Windstorm, CGC, TDI

Flavio v Dammerwald, SchH III, FH

Ch. Arras v Hasenkamp

Blanka vd Schachtschleuse, SchH I

Windstorm Still Storming

Ch. Kokas K's Degen v Burga, CD, TD

Windtara von Liebotschaner

Candlemas Tulip

Foxy's was established in 1979 with the aquisition of their foundation bitch an AKC Champion and Obedience titled producer. It has been our goal to breed top quality Rottweilers that possess the versatility to excel in obedience as well as the show ring. Seventeen years later, we are proud to present Ch. Foxy's Genesis V Windstorm, CGC, TDI. This spectacular dog is our third generation Champion Rottweiler. Rebel finished his American Championship by winning both his majors at Colonial Rottweiler Club supported shows. In Canada, Rebel has two five point majors and only needs a win to finish his Canadian Championship. Rebel is pictured above going BOW at Le Rottweiler Du Quebec Specialty!

Maria Fox
9227 Darlington Rd.
Philadelphia, PA 19115

Foxy's Rottweilers
(215) 934-5379

AM./PR./LA. Ch. ELKE VON EVMAN

Sire: Amboss Vom Konigssiek, SchH III, IPO III, Gekort

Dam: Ch. Cita Vom Glimmerfels

Elke started her career as the beautiful little girl you see here. Early in 1994 at only two years of age she was titled AKC's Number 1 Bitch.

1994	Nation's Number Two Bitch
1995	Westminster, Award of Merit
1996	Westminster, Best of Opposite Sex

Ron and Anne Yatteau
1824 Schriver Road
Knoxville, TN 37919

Touch of Class Rottweilers
(423) 584-9656, ayatteau @ aol.com

more serious fault, and what good points he values. Perhaps he will go with a dog which has no faults, but no outstanding features either. What is often taken as "crooked" judging is simply a matter of personal values on the part of the judge which may differ from those of the spectator or exhibitor. Remember, we do not ask a judge to tell us what he thinks is a perfect Rottweiler. We ask him his opinion in picking the best of what is in front of him that day! Like people, dogs may have good and bad days when they are more or less interested in showing. How well a dog LIKES to show is an important element, and gives him the "presence" he needs to be a winner.

There are no hard and fast rules about what constitutes a show dog. Any dog with an AKC number can be a show dog by paying the entry fee. If the dog has no disqualifying faults, he will be allowed to compete to the extent of completing his class. Some dogs are so average that they will consistently place under almost all judges, even in strong competition, but will never win. For although the dog has no faults, he has no great assets either. Others will win one day under a judge who appreciates the good qualities, and lose another day under a judge who puts emphasis on an area where the dog is weak. These dogs have an up and down career, but will probably still finish before the dog with no faults, but no great assets either.

Keep this in mind when you are buying a show dog, and keep it in mind when you are beginning to show. And remember what one of our breeders said: "A good judge is one who puts up my dog, a bad judge puts up someone else's dog, and a terrible judge puts up my worst enemy's dog!" What this means is that dog showing is a competitive sport. Over the years, exhibitors learn to appreciate certain things in a dog and dislike others. Breeders develop their own style within their kennel and dogs which are not of that style are "inferior" in their minds. But they are not the judge. The judge may agree with them one day, and disagree with them another day. All of this is to say that if you buy a dog, one of the worst things you can do is take it to a show and ask all the other exhibitors what they think of it. The opinions you get back are more likely to reflect the feelings of the individual exhibitor toward the style, and even the breeder of the dog, than they are to be an absolute evaluation of the dog.

If you are interested in showing, go to a show and see how your dog does in competition. If he wins, enjoy your success. If he loses several shows, consider that he may not be developed enough (if he is still immature) or that you might not be able to show him to his best advantage. Find a professional handler, and ask about him showing, or at least evaluating, your dog. These people handle a number of different breeds, from a wide variety of breeders. They know, overall, what a quality dog is and what it takes to get a dog finished. They are a more objective source of information than competing breeders or exhibitors.

Sometimes a judge will talk to you if you wait until after his assignment is over, though he is not required to do so and some do not like talking to exhibitors or novice owners. Sometimes a dog which cannot win as a puppy or young adult will mature into a fine show dog; he simply needs time to develop. Sometimes a dog can win in one geographic area of the country, but not another. This is because different geographic areas of the country are sometimes dominated by a particular style of Rottweiler. If all the dogs in the ring look alike, and yours looks different, he tends to look out of place. If shown in a different location, where he does not look so different, judges may be better able to appreciate his good qualities and he will win. The complexity of dog showing is one of the things that interests and fascinates people in the sport, and keeps them dedicated in time and money for many years.

Most breeders will not guarantee that a puppy will be a great show dog. They will sell a pup based on pedigree and what other, older siblings have done in the ring, and what the puppy looks like. The longer a breeder has bred and shown, the better idea he or she will have of how much POTENTIAL a pup has. But there are seldom guarantees because there are so many variables. The area of the country a dog shows in will make a difference in how fast he finishes. Who handles him, and how well he is conditioned and presented will make a difference. How much the dog ENJOYS showing will make a difference. And even experiences he has in the ring during his first few months of showing will make a difference.

Novice owners frequently take a young dog to a show, and when it does not win the first time or two, they begin to drag it around to other breeders and judges and inquire about its faults. This is very counterproductive, because all it does is call everyone's attention to

Schutzhund is a working title which involves obedience, protection and tracking work. It is designed to show the courage and working ability of the dog.

the negative aspects of the dog so that even when he does develop and would normally begin to win, everyone remembers the faults that have been pointed out early in the dog's career. Also remember, it is easier for people to make negative comments about a potential competitor than to recognize the good qualities and point out how to best set off the strengths. This is like asking a competing coach how to improve another team! And, if you have not bought a pup from the local breeders, they may resent the fact that they were overlooked when you went outside the area. Even if you bought your dog from a local breeder, other breeders in the area may comment on the dog (either in a negative or positive way) with more of an eye on how much they like the person who sold you the dog than on how nice the dog really is. More than one dog has been sent back to a breeder because the novice owner did not feel it was "show quality," and the breeder has finished it easily.

NEVER EXPECT ANYONE TO GUARANTEE THAT A PUPPY WILL BE A GROUP PLACING DOG. Group placings are dependent on so many different things, from the competition that day, to the early care a dog has received. Many people who want a group placing dog simply try to buy an older dog who has already started his show career and done well. Often handlers will find a dog they think has great promise and approach an owner about purchasing it. Sometimes, people who want a group placing dog will simply offer to "back" a dog which is already being shown and winning. This means that the "backer" puts his or her name on the dog and receives the fame for the dog's wins, and in return pays the bills to a greater or lesser extent, depending on the arrangement. Several top winning champions have been "owned" by backers who never bred or owned another dog of that breed, and who have no kennel and no intentions of ever breeding. When the dog was finished showing, he simply went back to the original owner who used him or her for breeding purposes, and gave the dog a home for the rest of its life.

OBEDIENCE

Show dogs have a career of one to four years. They will finish their championships, and if they are good, they will go on to show as champions against other champions. In three to four years they put on a little age, a little weight, and lose a little of their shine. While a few dogs can continue to show for longer than that, many of the top winners are retired from the ring by the time they are seven or eight years old.

By contrast, a working dog can continue to compete as long as he is able to move around in good health. With age, he may simply learn to do his job better. Rottweilers compete in a number of different competitions and do very well. Some dogs even learn to compete in several different ways, earning titles after they have retired from the show ring.

Obedience is another event at most dog shows. Unlike conformation showing where no special training is needed to start showing a young dog, obedience dogs are required to show off lead — that is, without a leash — and through a specific set of exercises. Judging is very precise. Scoring is done by subtracting points for faults such as failing to sit square, to return fully, or to stay in step on the heel exercise. Conformation dogs do not need to sit — in fact they should NOT sit while in the ring. Obedience dogs are required to sit when the handler stops walking, and when a command is given throughout the exercise program.

Obedience dogs need to have reached a level of training so that they can go through precise movements on the command of their handlers, including heel, sit, stay and down.

An obedience dog must be by nature intelligent and willing to please. Rottweilers do very well in obedience and you will see several of the dogs in our Hall of Fame with the letters CD, CDX or UD after their name. These letters represent "Companion Dog," Companion Dog Excellent" and "Utility Dog," the three levels of obedience competition, each in turn representing a more difficult level of performance. Conformation classes and obedience classes are held at the same time in different rings. This makes it very difficult, especially for a young dog and a novice handler, to adapt to the different types of showing, and work with the conflicting scheduling which often develops. You will usually find a dog which does either obedience or conformation, or a dog who has completed one title, then finishes an-

Rottweilers do very well in obedience and you will see a number of working titles after the names of dogs featured in our Hall of Fame.

other title, rather than finding many dogs who are entered in both conformation and obedience in the same show.

Dogs begin with the Novice class. A and B divisions relate to the handler. "A" dogs are handled by their owners, and only one dog may be shown in the class, while a "B" dog may be handled by his owner or by a professional handler or trainer. Several dogs may be handled by the same owner or handler in the same "B" class. There are six exercises which score points: Heel on Leash; Stand for Examination; Heel Free; Recall; Long Sit; Long Down, with a possible total of 200 points. All but the Heel on Leash must be done off lead, and a dog must score at least 50% of the available points in each exercise AND have a total score of 170 or higher in three obedience trials, at three different shows (with at least six dogs in competition) to earn a CD (Companion Dog) title. The dog may then move up to the next level of competition.

The second level has seven exercises. Each must be precisely executed. They are: Heel Free; Drop on Recall; Retrieve on Flat; Retrieve Over High Jump; Broad Jump; Long Sit; Long Down. Three qualifying scores at three different shows are needed to earn the title

of CDX. Dogs may then move up to Utility Dog competition to earn a UD title. This is the highest title an obedience dog can earn. The seven exercises include scent discrimination, hand signals, and both broad and high jumps. Rottweilers are surprisingly agile for their size and can usually jump very well.

Almost every show has classes for obedience. They are usually held in a ring apart from the conformation showing. If you are interested in showing your dog in obedience, begin with a local obedience class. Be prepared to work with him on

A Rottweiler working sheep. Recently people have become interested in using the breed in herding trials.

a daily basis for several months before you attempt to show. You may want to start showing at a local "match show." These are practice shows for both conformation and obedience. They offer no points toward a title, but they are usually small, with limited competition and no pressure and they are a good place to begin to learn the dog show game.

Conformation and obedience are two very different kinds of activities and they frequently attract different kinds of personalities. Even the dress is different. Handlers of obedience dogs wear casual clothes. Many obedience people feel that dark pants help them blend with the dog and minimize mistakes. Shirts and pants, even for women, are the normal attire. In conformation, especially in the East, women almost always wear dresses, suits with skirts, or skirts and blouses. Men wear sports coats and ties, except on very hot days when the judge may indicate that the coat may be disregarded. Men are seldom seen without a tie, jeans are not appropriate, and women are almost never seen in pants. In California and some other areas, golf shirts and pants are sometimes worn, though jeans and T-shirts are never considered appropriate.

AGILITY

Begun in 1977 in England, Agility is an obstacle course for dogs. It is fun, fast and growing in popularity each year. Dogs go through a series of obstacles, over a bridge, across teeter totters, through tunnels and barrels, between poles, and over A-frames.

Dogs must be over 6 months old, and able to compete through obstacles off lead. Dogs compete against time over the obstacles and lose points for failing to complete an obstacle as described. Qualifying scores add toward titles, but high score dogs at an event are also recognized. Call your local kennel club for details on Agility Clubs in your area. Most kennel clubs have at least a few members who are interested or active in agility and new clubs are forming every year.

Although demonstrations are sometimes held in conjunction with AKC conformation shows, most agility competitions are held as separate events, involving dogs of different breeds. Different classes, depending on the level of training for the dogs and handlers, are offered. Classes are also divided by the different size breeds so that a Rottweiler must go over larger obstacles than a Dachshund. The atmosphere is casual and the event usually progresses throughout the day, with scores and times posted after the events so people can see how they have done.

For those who are very interested, there is a National Championship. A dog must qualify to compete, and for many years these finals have been held in Houston, Texas, and have attracted dogs from all over the country and in almost all breeds.

AKC CANINE GOOD CITIZEN TEST AND TEMPERAMENT TESTING

Recently, the AKC has recognized the need for responsible dog ownership and promotion of well trained dogs. This has given rise to a new event, the Canine Good Citizen test. Most clubs put on a CGC test at least once a year. This test lasts most of a day, and all breeds of dogs are tested, though they are evaluated one at a time. This event tests the dog's ability to do basic obedience and his attitude in meeting new people and new situations. If he passes the test, he is awarded a CGC title. These tests are growing in popularity and more and more dogs are showing up with CGC attached to their names.

Temperament Testing is somewhat similar, though it is not done through AKC. These tests require a dog to meet friendly strangers, hostile strangers, neutral strangers, and a variety of situations. Again, the test will take up the better part of a day. The title earned will stay with the dog for life. You will see a number of dogs in the Hall of Fame with CGC or TT at the end of their name. This indicates that they have entered and passed one of these competitions.

TRACKING

Another AKC performance test is Tracking. Since it inception in the 1930's, tracking events have been a performance test for many breeds. The first level of accomplishment is the TD, or "Tracking Dog." The advanced level, offered since 1947, is the TDX, or "Tracking Dog Excellent." You will see that title at the end of the name of several of the dogs listed in the Hall of Fame. These tests measure the ability of the dog to do what dogs have done since they helped prehistoric hunters track game. Rottweilers have enjoyed a lot of success in this area, and the events are usually less formal than shows. Many of the events are part of large Rottweiler Specialty weekends across the country and are interesting to watch even if you are not ready to compete.

Tracking will test you and your dog as a team. You will need a harness, a twenty to thirty foot lead and enough material to make six to eight flags. It will take roughly the same amount of time to train for a TD as it does to train for a CD, and it is something which will be a challenge to both you and your dog. A dog must pass the Tracking Test under two different judges to earn a TD.

During the competition, which is usually held in an area isolated from frequent disturbances such as a dog show, dogs are required to follow the scent of a trail previously laid down for the purposes of the trial. These competitions are open to dogs six months of age or older, and a dog may continue to compete even after he has earned his title. There is a catalog listing the names of the dogs in competition and alternates, and the number of dogs which can compete on any given day is limited. Entries are made in advance, and after entries close, a lottery is held to determine the order. If there are more entries than are allowed by the published limit, preference is given to dogs who have not yet earned their titles, and a lottery is held to see which dogs will be allowed to compete. Alternates are also chosen.

For the TD level, a track at least 440 yards is set. The length of each of the "legs," or straight sections of the track, are to be at least 50 yards, so the trail cannot be a mass of twists and turns. The track is laid down at least thirty minutes — and no more than two hours before the dog competes. The track makes three to five turns, two of which must be at least 90°, and they must go both to the right and to the left. These tests are held outdoors, over a variety of terrain, so each competition is different.

The TDX competition is similar, but the tracks are more difficult. There are also other independent clubs and associations which put on tracking competitions. These competitions are somewhat different than the AKC tracking events, run under different rules, and award different titles. Another competition called the Variable Surface Tracking Test is open to dogs who have earned their TD title. The title VST is awarded to those who successfully complete the requirements.

CARTING

Another enjoyable competition is carting. Several breeds including Newfoundlands, Saint Bernards, Great Pyrenees and Bouvier des Flandres have competed in carting competitions for many years. Recently, Rottweilers have begun to go back to their ancestral use as draft dogs. It is relatively simple to teach your Rottweiler to pull a cart, and he will enjoy it if properly approached. Once your dog is fully mature and has sound basic obedience behavior down, you can start. Be sure he is confident and of solid temperament, and take things slowly. With a well-fitting harness and a cart you can not only be in competition at a number of specialties around the country, but you can have your Rottweiler helping around the house, carting his own dog food from the car to the storage area, helping with gardening by carrying plants and potting soil, or taking the kids for a ride through the park. One breeder notes, her cart-trained dog pulls his own crate and show equipment from the car to the setup area at shows! Some Rottweiler Specialties have begun to include carting competitions.

HERDING

Rottweilers also shine in Herding competitions. With natural herding instincts, many will take to the training easily. Several Rottweilers have been respected herders and have held titles under the American Herding Breeds Association (AHBA). Recently, AKC has included Rottweilers in herding trials. Herding Rottweilers show good control of the livestock and are thoughtful workers, often tending to be quieter, both in style and in vocalization than some of the more traditional herding breeds.

SCHUTZHUND

Finally, yet not by any means the least important competition is the "Schutzhund" competition, a working title earned under the United Schutzhund Clubs of America. This is a completely separate organization from AKC; it comprises over 150 full member clubs and over a dozen more affiliated clubs. These clubs are comprised of more than 4,000 members.

Schutzhund competition is very serious, and takes a good deal of time and training. Although there is great joy and satisfaction from a well working Schutzhund team, it takes dedication and a concerted effort to educate yourself in training before you undertake to work with your dog. Find an expert and attend some trials. Understand what you are doing before you begin to work with your dog. Schutzhund is a German word meaning "protection dog." It refers to a sport that focuses on developing and evaluating those traits in dogs that make them more useful to man. The protection phase is based heavily on police dog work, while the obedience phase simply requires a solid temperament and basic obedience training. The exercises are designed to measure mental stability, endurance, sound structure, courage and trainability. In Germany, dogs recommended for breeding must pass a series of inspections and accomplishment.

Schutzhund work is fascinating and a challenge. However, in many parts of Europe, a Schutzhund trained dog is considered a weapon. Be sure you know what you are doing before undertaking to train your dog for this kind of work. Seek out competent instruction for both you and your dog and be sure you completely understand the art of Schutzhund before you begin.

There are three parts of a Schutzhund Trial: tracking, obedience and protection. The levels, or titles which can be earned, are Schutzhund I, II and III. You will see a number of dogs in the Hall of Fame with these titles, abbreviated SchH I, II, and III. Each level is more difficult, but each contains elements of all three parts. The tracking phase includes work at the end of a thirty-foot leash. The dog follows a trail laid down previously by a stranger. Each level is more difficult. For example, a level I dog must be fourteen months old and be able to follow a track at least twenty minutes old. A level II dog follows a trail at least thirty minutes old, and a level III dog follows a trail at least fifty minutes old. Level II dogs must be at least sixteen months old, and level III dogs must be at least eighteen months old. Each level has a track which is more complex, with more turns, and the dog must find several objects which are laid down by the stranger and to identify them, usually by lying down with the object between the front paws.

The obedience phase is much like AKC obedience. A dog is expected to work off lead, sit, stay, and come on recall. In addition, the dog retrieves on the flat, over a jump and over an A-frame wall. During the heel, a gun is fired to test the dog's assurance and reactions to sharp noise.

Finally, the protection phase of the trial tests the dog's courage and physical strength. It includes attacking a subject. Human decoys are used. These people, wearing specially designed padded "sleeves," act much like a suspect would act in police custody. To stop an "escape" the dog is expected to grip the suspect firmly and without hesitation, but he is also expected to release on command or as soon as the decoy discontinues resistance. The dog is to be neither a coward nor a criminal menace.

This working sport offers an opportunity for dog owners to train their dogs and compete with each other for recognition of both the handler's ability to train and the dog's ability to perform as required. It is a sport enjoyed by all ages and from a wide variety of professions.

SHIPPING AND TRAVEL

*T*he first opportunity a puppy has to travel is when he goes to his new home. In some cases, you may not be able to find the kind of dog you are looking for locally. It is more important to find the right dog than to locate something fast or close. If you have a choice of driving eight or ten hours, or flying a dog, flying is an option to think about. Although some of our breeders were very much against flying, many reported that puppies travel very well, and several indicated that they felt a flight was less stress on a pup than a long drive. When flying, the pup usually goes to sleep with the sound of the engines, waking when he arrives at his destination. By contrast, a long drive in a car, involves temperature and water changes, strange potty stops where the pup may be exposed to viruses, lack of exercise and motion which may cause car sickness. It is very common for pups to get car sick and not get air sick.

Flying a puppy in is relatively easy. A puppy may not fly until it is eight weeks old. Shipping should take place after the first set of shots have been given. The cost is $70-$110 for the flight, and $25-$55 for the crate. A dog may not be shipped if the temperature is below 30 degrees, or higher than 90 degrees. If the pup goes freight, you may pay for the flight and even the crate (if you purchase it from the airlines) collect, at the time you pick up your pup at the airport. Airlines use a top-of-the-line crate and there are several good, less expensive crates on the market which are still safe and airline approved, but at half the cost. This crate will only be useful for a puppy, since a full grown Rottweiler will need a much larger crate. The breeder will drop the puppy off at the freight office of the airline, and you will pick him up at the freight office.

If the pup flies counter to counter, the freight must be paid when the dog is put on the plane. The advantage to this method is that the temperature restrictions are much less rigid since the puppy is hand carried to the plane and loaded with the baggage. Less time is needed between flights if the dog must make a connecting flight, and the dog is dropped off and picked up at the ticket counter with oversized baggage. However, there is a size and weight limit on this type of shipping and only smaller puppies will qualify.

Although there are some stories of dogs being mishandled or dying during shipping, one breeder said she has shipped dogs over half of a million air miles over the years, and never had a problem. We could not find a single breeder who had directly experienced a real trauma with airlines. While some breeds of dogs have breathing or respiratory problems which make them poor shipping risks, Rottweilers will generally settle in for the ride.

If you have picked up your pup at the airport, bring him directly home; do not use that opportunity to visit friends and show him off. He needs to see his new home, have time and quiet to get adjusted, and to get food and water. Although the airlines require food and water dishes, most breeders will not send food or water with the pup. A full stomach can lead to airsickness, and water bowls tip as the crate is carried and leave the bedding wet and cold. Bring the pup home, let him inspect the new area, give him a bed, food and water immediately. With a full stomach and a little quiet, he will be himself in a short time. It will probably take a day or two for him to settle in and become the normal, active puppy he was when he left his litter.

The next time your dog will have a chance to fly might be on vacation with you. Check the dog in as excess luggage and it will fly with you for a minimal cost. Shipping a full grown Rottweiler usually requires a #400 or #500 crate, and may be expensive. Be prepared to pay about $160 for a one-way trip. For that reason, bitches being bred to dogs out of the area often make use of frozen semen, which can go in overnight mail or ship counter to counter as medical supplies.

Dogs may not travel on trains. But they do adapt easily to new places if they have been raised properly, and they can become good, solid travelers. They travel well in motor homes for a change of pace family vacation, and Rottweilers are usually be happy to see new surroundings and to take long hikes in the wilderness after you arrive. A walk in a new city can also be of interest to them!

If you are staying in hotels, most of our breeders offer one word of advice: CRATE. Crate train your dog, and bring the crate on vacation with you. Some hotels will accept a crated dog, while they have learned not to accept dogs which may be left on their own in hotel rooms, bored, upset and ready to do damage that these perfect pets would never think of doing at home. A crate is not necessarily a bad thing to a dog. For him, it is a part of his home which has come with him and gives him a feeling of stability. The crate can help him stay calm and get some sleep while you go out to dinner or to see sights where a dog may not be allowed. A hotel room with a crate is certainly safer and better than locking him in a hot car.

If you are traveling with your dog, be sure to bring plenty of food and water, bowls for food and water, and a leash. Even a dog that stays around the house is likely to become excited and disoriented in a strange place and a leash is good insurance to keep him from wandering into traffic or getting lost. Other helpful items to travel with are Pepto Bismol tablets in case he gets hold of something that gives him diarrhea, Dramamine for carsickness (especially if it is a young dog who has not ridden in a car often), Benadryl for possible reactions to insect bites and flea spray, especially if you are near the beach. Having these things with you when you need them can take some of the stress out of travel.

If you are traveling by car with a puppy, take a few precautions to help make the trip easier. Do not feed him for an hour or so before you leave. Take him for a walk right before departure so that he has every opportunity to relieve himself while he still has the chance. Take along a box, bed or cage that he is used to so that something familiar will accompany him, much like bringing along a stuffed animal or blanket for a child. Don't let him travel with his head out the window, as he can get grit or wind in his eyes which may trigger entropion. And, it is unsafe because he does not have the intelligence to realize that the car is traveling at speed and he may suddenly try to jump out. Stop every few hours to let him get a drink of water, get some exercise and relieve himself. But be sure to keep him on a leash so that he does not dart out in front of a car or approach a strange dog.

Never let your pup approach a strange dog. Rottweilers will seldom back down, even as pups. If the strange dog challenges him, and the pup becomes defensive, the other dog may react too quickly for you to prevent serious injury to the puppy.

In hot weather, a crate is a necessity. Never leave a dog in the car, but if you are going somewhere such as a picnic or a baseball game, take the crate out of the car, place it in the shade, and the dog can safely be left without worrying about overheating. Rottweilers, like all black dogs, are more susceptible to heat stroke in direct sun, or in a car. Rottweilers, as a breed, do not tolerate the heat well. Heat stroke is one of the leading causes of death in well loved dogs — be careful during summer months.

If you are traveling and intend to leave the dog at home, you have three choices. You can kennel your dog, leave him in the care of a friend or relative, or set up some kind of care for him in your home. A kennel is the safest and easiest way to care for your dog when you are away. Rottweilers often do not like strangers and many of our breeders felt they did better in a kennel where strangers left them alone, than in the home of a friend or family member they did not know well. Other pets already in the other home may also be a problem, as some Rottweilers are animal aggressive, especially without their families, and especially if challenged. By contrast, they will survive a kennel trip well if it is a reputable, clean kennel and they can have their own area and the chance to stay by themselves until the owner returns.

If you are counting on someone coming into the house to feed and care for your pet, be sure that the caretaker is reliable. Many areas of the country have professional "pet sitters." These people come into the home, check on pets and care for them, and keep an eye on the house at the same time. Professional pet sitters offer the advantage of keeping the dog at home where he feels comfortable, while at the same time there is someone in and out of the house and the dog is there to watch out for intruders. The success of this option depends on how secure your yard (or the area where the dog is to be housed) is. For example, if there is a yard or pool man going in or out there is a possibility the dog will slip out the gate. If the fencing is not secure, or the shelter not good, this is not a good alternative. Finally, the reliability of the pet sitter is a concern. Friends or sitters who are not well recommended may be too busy to come by on a regular basis, and the dog may be at risk because if something goes wrong, it may go undetected. Many breeders recommend that you try this type of arrangement before you leave. Rottweilers are good protectors of their homes, and sometimes, even with people they know, they refuse to let the temporary caretaker into the home!

TRAINING

*I*f you are going to own a Rottweiler, take on the responsibility of training him from the beginning. There has been a lot of unfavorable publicity about the breed in the last few decades and as a responsible member of the community, it is your duty to be sure your dog does not contribute to that image. No matter how nice his temperament, the Rottweiler is a large dog, and without proper training and socialization, may be difficult to contain. The mental health of your dog depends on the type and consistency of training you put into him. As with a child, you are helping to mold his character. To a large extent, how well he fits into your family when he is an adult depends on the values you instill in him as a puppy and young adult.

First, time is a necessary ingredient. If you turn him out in a run or in the backyard and never have time for him, he will become wild and uncontrollable. Rottweilers love their families and need time to develop a bond. Quality time is no substitute for quantity, though the quality of the time you spend with him is important.

Second, your attitude is of utmost importance. You must strive to *mentally* dominate your Rottweiler. Making your presence known to him, making him understand what you will tolerate and what you will not tolerate is NOT a matter of physical domination. To physically dominate a Rottweiler is difficult to begin with. They are large and powerful dogs. To physically dominate the dog will lead to problems which are unpleasant at best and dangerous at worst. A dog which behaves out of fear often becomes an unpredictable "fear biter."

The dam begins the puppy's training in the whelping box. When she is displeased with his behavior she will growl, shoving him with her muzzle or snapping at him if the behavior continues. Like his mother, a voice of displeasure, a sharply barked command, or a stern verbal reprimand will produce the desired effect in most cases. Begin with the command "NO," which roughly means, "Whatever you are doing, stop it!" In some cases, your pup may already have a basic knowledge of that command by the time he arrives at your home. If not, be sure it is the first thing you teach him. If he fails to obey, a rap on the nose with a finger, or physically picking him up and giving him a short shake will do the trick.

Our breeders differ on discipline. Some think that a smack on the bottom is better than a finger on the nose, saying that a rap on the nose will make the dog hand shy. Others believe that the dog does not pay any attention to the smack on bottom. Rottweilers are stout dogs who do not pay attention to minor physical annoyances! These breeders say they have never seen any indication that a dog will become hand shy from a rap on the nose. In either case, the command and the reprimand should be short, firm and nonabusive. The idea is to stop the undesirable behavior, not to intimidate the dog.

Firm verbal commands and consistent, fair treatment should be the goal. People who are confident and stable in their own personalities will raise a dog which is confident and stable. If you are flighty or nervous, the Rottweiler is probably not the breed for you. Constant nagging and punishment which is drawn out only confuses a dog and makes him resentful instead of sensitive to when you are displeased. Remember also, that in order to make it important to him that he pleases you, he must KNOW when he pleases you. Praise is an important and necessary ingredient.

One of the tricks to mental domination is to be able to outmaneuver the dog so that you never get into direct confrontation. Switching a favorite toy for a shoe you do not wish the puppy to chew on gives you the shoe, and keeps you from simply pulling the shoe away from him. It is natural that the puppy will feel that the shoe is a prize, and he will try to take it back as a natural reaction. If you say "NO," take the shoe and give him the toy, he will learn the lesson and be sidetracked to the toy instead of concentrating on getting the prize back.

Learning his name is another early lesson. The puppy has probably learned to come to a general puppy call for food, or to come in for the evening. Simply continue that by calling his name when you feed him. Although some of our breeders do not believe in treats to reward behavior, many of our breeders feel that this is a perfectly natural and acceptable practice. Rottweilers are naturally "greedy" and appreciative of rewards in the form of treats. As long as the treat is accepted with proper control, not snapped out of the hand of the handler, it seems reasonable to many that the dog should get a reward for proper behavior.

Next, a puppy should learn to walk on a leash early in his life. The idea of trying to leash train a full grown Rottweiler is much more absurd than trying to leash train a full grown Toy Poodle, for example! Put the collar on the puppy and simply let him walk around. Some of them will be convinced that they cannot move another inch until the collar comes off, while others are not concerned in the slightest and take little notice of what is hanging around their neck. Attach the leash, and simply follow the dog around for a while, going where he wants to go. You can increase your command over the situation by talking, playing or offering a treat to change the puppy's direction, or to make him follow you. Be sure that the lessons are short, and that he can always succeed in achieving what you want to teach him that day. Never quit on a bad note. If he will not follow you, reconstruct the exercise so that you are asking him to do something you can get him to do. Then praise his efforts and quit for the day. Always break the task down into small parts that he can understand and make it as fun as possible.

A well mannered Rottweiler is a wonderful companion, a good neighbor, and a faithful friend. For a well adjusted, well trained adult you must begin with a well bred dog with intelligence and a solid temperament, and as an owner, you must invest time in training him from the time he is a puppy.

By the time he is six months old and ready for obedience classes, he should have some basis of understanding basic commands such as his name, "No," how to walk on a leash, and how to know when you are pleased and when you are not pleased. If you have taken him out and about on a regular basis, the noise, confusion and other dogs in the obedience class should not frighten him. Obedience classes in some areas of the country are crowded and there may be a waiting list. Breeders often recommend that you investigate these classes immediately upon purchasing a puppy so that you will be at the top of the waiting list by the time the puppy is six months old and ready to begin more formal training.

Remember, never let a puppy do anything you do not want a full grown Rottweiler to do. Behaviors which are cute on a Miniature Pinscher, or even a Cocker Spaniel, may not be as cute in a dog weighing over one hundred pounds. Jumping up to say "hello," is an example. Other examples are running after anything that moves, and grabbing at the feet of human friends. Many Rottweilers, perhaps because of their herding instincts, have a tendency to run and grab at moving objects, from people to bicycles and cars. Some have a stronger instinct for this than others, but it is sufficient to say that this is probably NOT going to be a popular behavior for a full grown Rottweiler. Correct it while the puppy is young with firm, immediate correction.

Another habit you will have to decide about is mouthing. Many breeds have a tendency to approach a loved one and to take the hand or arm in their mouths. It begins with playful puppy biting, and the puppy's natural inclination — like that of a human baby — to test the environment by gripping and holding. But many older dogs will do it out of affection. To anyone who has not had contact with a breed that is prone to this behavior, and Rottweilers are one of those breeds, it can be a little alarming. Decide early in the puppy's life if you will accept this and realize he will probably continue this "mouthing" as affection into adulthood. It is not simply a function of teething. If the practice is acceptable, fine. If you have reservations, or are worried that there is a fine line between "love" and "dominance," you should stop the practice before it becomes a habit.

Part of the successful bond between child and dog involves not only training the dog, but teaching the child to respect and care for the animal.

Dominance is important to a Rottweiler. Some breeders discourage such "games" as wrestling with the dog. Males, especially those in their adolescent stage, will consider this not a game, but a test of superiority. Remember, games and play are a way of life to a dog. He does not go out to school or a job every day and come home, ready to distinguish recreation from the more serious parts of life! When the play become too rough, or the human becomes bored or tired, the game is ended. The human considers it the end of the game, but the dog may well believe that he has successfully dominated the situation, and taken a step toward dominating the relationship. The same is true for "tug of war" toys. The dog pulls one end, the human the other. It is the human who lets go first. To the dog, this is another victory. Toys which can be thrown and retrieved are much more valuable in developing a bond without creating aggression.

Many people who purchase a Rottweiler do so because they want a dog for protection.

All too often, they encourage aggression with commands like, "Sic him," or "Go get him," applauding the dog's natural aggressive tendencies. A Rottweiler will guard your home and his family by nature. He does not need encouragement. Work on control, on being able to stop the aggression on command when the dog has not interpreted the situation correctly. You are the responsible, intelligent party of the household, YOU should make the decision when aggression is proper and when it is not. If you continually encourage aggressive behavior at the whim of the dog, you will be laying the groundwork for a potentially dangerous situation. OUR BREEDERS EMPHASIZE OVER AND OVER AGAIN that the KEY to owning a protective guard dog is control and training. None of our breeders want to see their dogs go into homes where aggression is encouraged to the point where the dog gets into a situation where he could be considered aggressive, out of control or dangerous. In any situation where the dog makes an error in judgment about when and under what circumstances to attack, the dog suffers, in some cases with his life!!

In our chapter on competitions and other things you can do with your Rottweiler, we discuss some of the activities your dog can participate in, including Schutzhund training. We would like to inject one word of caution. "Guard Dog" training is a serious matter. If you intend to become involved in this aspect of dogs, be informed of all of the consequences. We have a number of breeders in the Hall of Fame who will encourage your participation. We also have a number of breeders who feel very strongly *against* using a dog in this way. Be sure to talk to your breeder BEFORE you purchase a puppy to learn more about protection work, and the suitability of your puppy for this kind of training.

If you are interested in Schutzhund work, please understand the seriousness of what you are creating. ***This is NOT a backyard procedure.*** In some countries this type of work requires a license and is looked upon as if the handler is creating a weapon. Take the time and energy to find a good trainer who knows what he is doing, and do not attempt to read a book and try it at home without experience in the field. Understand what you are doing, not just from the surface performance which is obvious, but to understand the techniques and the way a dog thinks about training. Talk to people in the field, preferably more than one authority, and then proceed with intelligence, care and understanding — ***NEVER as a home project.*** It is extremely important to get CORRECT BEHAVIOR, not simply approximate behavior!

BREEDING YOUR DOG -
WHY THIS MIGHT NOT BE SUCH A GOOD IDEA!

*N*ow that you have your dog, you may entertain the idea that you should breed it. If you read one of the larger books on the breed, or one of the many dog books that discuss breeding, they discuss genetics and how to build a whelping box, and they make it sound easy. On the other hand, breeders and breed associations will say that you "should not breed your dog." That makes it sound like an ethical decision on a higher plane, and you may be tempted to simply say, "But I just want one litter, what could it hurt?" Here is probably the most honest evaluation of why this may be one of the many times in life when something LOOKS better on the outside than it does when you actually TRY it.

Have you ever gone somewhere and seen a WONDERFUL layout of model trains or a large doll house? The hobby looked fascinating and easy. You may have even gone out

and bought a small doll house, or a starter set of trains. Then you began to discover just how much time and money really went into this simple looking project. You needed space to work on the project, and space to set it up. You needed special tools and materials you had never worked with before, and they were all expensive. You had to spend time shopping for the right pieces of the right size so that it all went together. And the pieces that went into it were expensive. Very quickly you found that this seemingly simple setup was going to cost you hours and hours of your life and hundreds of dollars just to get off to a good start. And when you put together the first pieces, it was a boring, poor substitute for the intricate, fascinating set up you had seen. In the end you gave up on it, losing the money you might have invested in the train set which is now on a shelf in the garage, or the doll house which still remains without those hundreds of maddening little shingles pasted to the roof! In short, your time and money were not well spent unless you found it to be something you were interested in to the point where you became involved and dedicated!

Like all hobbies, there is much more to dog breeding than first meets the eye. Enthusiasts put time and money into this, just as with any hobby. And the result which looks simple is the product of careful planning and investment. To do it in any way short of that kind of planning will result in something far short of the goal, which is a waste of your time and money. And even a single litter can consume much more time and money than you ever imagined when you began the project.

In 1994, 31,1476 LITTERS of Rottweilers were registered with AKC. This is up from 1992, when 28,551 litters were registered. But the most interesting thing is that only about three and one third Rottweilers are registered per litter. Our breeders reported that an average litter is seven to nine pups. This means that there are almost three times as many Rottweilers whelped every year as are registered. These "left over" dogs usually go to pet homes, and often the owners never bother to register them. Some of them will find their way into the breeding population, being bred to local dogs, to produce low quality Rottweilers, which will find their way into the local newspapers. With that kind of population, it is no wonder that the breed has suffered in quality, health and temperament. All Rottweilers are simply NOT alike!

Most people decide to breed their dog for one of the following reasons: A) it looks like easy money. Call a few breeders, find out the price of pups, and the number of pups in

a litter, and the profit doesn't look bad. But remember, you are playing the *Kibbles and Bits Slot Machine.* You may make money on a litter here and there, but there is a greater potential to lose money, sanity, friends, and routine. The odds are better at Las Vegas. How much stress is it worth to you to make a few dollars? How many nice things in your home will end up with tooth marks? And like any new business venture, there is AL-WAYS investment before there is profit. How much are you willing to invest before you have a payoff?

B) People think that it would be a wonderful experience for the children. Buy a video! It's cheaper, cleaner, less stressful, and the kids will learn more. The kids will play with the pups for a few days and then go back to Nintendo or outside to play ball, depending on their interests. A litter of eight week old pups is too young to have manners enough to stay away from Nintendo controls, but too small to play with the kids! In the end, the kids may find the pups more annoying than interesting. It is like having eight toddlers around the house. One of our breeders said she remembered her children taking the pups out of the puppy pen, then getting interested in something else and forgetting about the pups, leaving unhousetrained pups prying into every corner of the house unsupervised!

C) You may decide you want a second dog. Friends and family have said they also wanted a dog. But frequently, friends who have repeatedly said, "If you ever breed Hilda, we want a pup," will be the first to tell you AFTER the litter is eight weeks old and you have asked them when they are going to get their puppy that they "...really can't take a puppy this time, but for sure the next time you breed her!"

D) There may be no decision at all. A neighborhood male jumps the fence. (Yes, even six footers have been known to be scaled.) The bitch slipped out past the kids when she was in season. No one realized that she was in season. The list goes on and on. It is much easier to get an accidental breeding than you can ever imagine. Mixed litters are the hardest to get rid of, and you have all the disadvantages of raising a litter, with none of the advantages of producing a nice puppy, or being able to sell it. For this reason, we highly recommend that you SPAY ANY BITCH YOU DID NOT BUY FOR THE EXPRESS PURPOSE OF BREEDING.

If you bought your dog as a pet, you may find that you have a limited registration, which means that your pups are not eligible for registration. The breeder, with his knowledge of genetics, may have priced your dog as a pet and found a pet home for her because for some reason he did not feel that puppies should be produced from her.

When you consider breeding your dog, think about some very important factors.

First, did you buy a nice quality dog, from a good breeder? Is this a dog the breeder himself would want to breed? If the answer is "NO," don't breed your dog just to get a litter of puppies. It is this kind of breeding that lowers the quality of the Rottweiler and gives the breed a bad name. If you did not make it clear that you were looking for a breeding bitch at the time of purchase, the chances are that your bitch is not of breeding quality. This goes back to the necessity of making it very clear WHAT you want the dog for at the time of purchase, and being willing to pay a good price for good quality. There may be hidden genetic problems that the breeder knows are in your dog — ones that will not affect her life and health, but which may appear in her puppies. The breeder may not have explained this to you because you said all you wanted was a pet. As long as YOUR dog was not affected, there was no reason for the breeder to go into it. But if you breed the dog, it will surely appear again, and then YOU are the breeder who has to deal with the problem. You are the one who has to deal with puppy buyers upset over problems with their puppies. And you are the one who must agree to replace a puppy with a problem, or be prepared and knowledgeable enough to help the new owner cope with the situation.

Second, even though there are a lot of dogs in the newspaper every week, remember that with all of the Rottweilers out there, it may not be as easy as it looks to sell the pups. It is one thing to look at a litter of eight pups and say to yourself, "Even at $300 each, that is $2,400!" and another to reap that kind of profit. The road is filled with pitfalls, chewed furniture, expenses that add up like a city street repair budget, and more work than being coach of the Little League team!

It may sound like a jackpot. You appear to do nothing, and extra pocket money comes rolling in! But think about the expenses you incur. You have to build or buy a box for her to whelp and raise the pups in or she will pick the bed, a closet (after she has pulled all of the clothes off the hangers to make her own bed) or the middle of the flower bed. Pups need shots and worming. Even if your vet is very reasonable, $70 is the lowest you will pay ($25 for the office call and $5 per pup). It is time consuming to take the pups to the vet.

You have the expense of the puppy food, and the additional food the bitch will require during the time she is carrying and nursing. Eight or nine pups will consume an alarming amount of high priced puppy food.

Advertising in the local newspaper will run at least $20 to $40 per weekend. Count the number of Rottweiler ads in your newspaper. The odds are that you will not be able to sell the entire litter in one week end. It will take you three or four AT BEST. You will have to stay home to answer the phone, and you will have at least a dozen strangers coming to your home to see the pups. Rottweilers are cute pups and there are the inevitable "window shoppers." The price of two or three pups will be needed JUST TO COVER THE EXPENSE YOU HAVE IN RAISING THE LITTER AND SELLING IT.

And here are some other things that can go wrong: There is the expense and trouble of the breeding. Either one pup or a stud fee is usually paid to the owner of the stud, even if he is a local dog. Stud fees on known dogs run around $500 to $1,000. If you have chosen a dog that is not within driving distance, you will need to ship the bitch, or the semen. Shipping the frozen semen is easier, but then you must pay a vet, or someone who is authorized to make the breeding by inseminating the bitch.

If you are breeding to a good stud, you will have to plan ahead to book the breeding. It is best to start that BEFORE the bitch comes in season. You will need to send a copy of your bitch's pedigree and perhaps her picture to the owner of the stud for approval in most cases. When it is time for breeding, you will have to get a current brucellosis test. Although uncommon, brucellosis is a contagious disease which is usually sexually transmitted between dogs. It can be contagious to humans from handling the dogs during breeding or whelping, and there is some new evidence to show it can also be transmitted between dogs through waste material. Rather than risk it, most breeders will require a current brucellosis certificate. A test from six months or a year before is not considered current. Many breeders will also require hip and eye certification. These tests can eat up the price of two to three more pups.

There are often problems with a sale. Someone buys a pup, and it gets sick, and they want YOU to pay the vet bill. Or, they can't keep it and want to bring it back. Someone brings in a virus and the litter gets sick and you have hundreds of dollars of vet bills — it happens all the time. Even the best breeders have problems with a virus in a litter from time to time.

As the pups begin to move around, they may get out of their area and chew up furniture or kitchen cabinets. The force of a litter of wiggling, happy, uncontrollable seven week old puppies is enough to move such things as baby gates and temporary pens, and scratch up back doors. Outside, these little fellows will dig and chew up bushes unless you have a specific pen built for them. Now we are into the expense of building a place to contain them between the time the bitch has had enough, and when you can sell them. This could be the longest month of your life! You must think of a way to begin to house train the litter, and spend the time to socialize them so that people coming to look at the pups are not met with wild pups, unused to human handling.

And winter puppies, inside because of the cold weather, will shred papers, take down barriers, and literally create several pounds of wet and soiled papers a day. Mopping and scraping smeared puppy poop will become a way of life! Certainly there are crates and cages called "puppy play pens" which do a very good job containing puppies and eliminating some of the mess. But they will run in the neighborhood of $140 each and will take up a space of about 4' X 4' in some inconvenient place in your home! In addition, they have wire floors which splay feet and break down the pasterns of heavy Rottweiler pups, and you will need two for a litter of eight pups.

In short, many people breed a litter because they think it is easy money, they want the "experience" of having a litter (which is a little like wanting to have the experience of juggling eight bowling balls without dropping them on your foot!) or because they want the kids to have the fun of a litter. They may want a second dog and this looks like a way to get one for themselves, friends, or family members.

By the time you add up expenses, it is cheaper to simply buy a nice second dog, and let your friends and relatives do the same. If they like your dog, give them the name of your breeder!

And perhaps this is the time to mention that the odor of your home may change, and friends may be less inclined to visit. Whelping has a distinctive smell. Amniotic fluid is dark green, stains whatever it comes in contact with, and has a permeating fragrance. Although the bitch will clean up after the litter when they are very young, her housekeeping may be somewhat lax when they get older and start on solid food. One of our breeders said she bought a breadmaking machine so that the aroma of yeast and fresh bread would fill the house, instead of the aroma of puppies!

Time is another thing you will need. When it is time to breed your bitch, you will need to drop everything and get it done. Putting it off until the weekend will often be too late. Veterinarians are often way off in their predictions of when to breed. They go by the book, and the bitch has not read the book! Keep in close contact with the breeder who knows what to expect, and make arrangements as soon as possible using their guidelines. If neither you nor the stud owner know what you are doing, be warned that Rottweilers are large and sometimes difficult to handle during breeding. *Someone should be experienced* in dog breeding, know what problems may arise, and what to do about them. Nature is not as reliable as you may imagine. At best, the breeding may not be successful, at worst the dog or bitch may be injured.

Are you prepared to stay home when the bitch is ready to whelp? Just as Murphy's Law predicts, the bitch is guaranteed to whelp in the middle of a dinner party, or on the day you have an important appointment — even if she has to be days early or days late to do it! The need of Caesarean Sections is always a possibility in Rottweilers, even though they are generally free whelpers. That leads to even more time and expense. First time bitches are often poor or confused mothers who do not clean pups well, or who step on pups. You should always be present at a whelping, especially on a first time bitch, or risk losing pups and/or the dam.

After they are born, you will need to start handling the pups from the beginning. Watch for poor nursers. Sometimes you will need to physically put a puppy which is nursing slowly, or who is getting shoved out of a big litter, on the teat and hold him on until he can get his fill. And there is always the chance that one or more of the pups will need tube or bottle feeding at least as a supplement. There is the time you will need to take them to the vet's for shots, and the time you will need to spend with them just getting them used to people and being handled. You will need to educate yourself about early socialization training, such as rolling the pups on their back. (Do you know why this is appropriate? If not, consider it just one of the things you do not know and learn more about breeding from an experienced breeder before you try it.)

And there is the inevitable cleanup time. When the litter gets older, they will be glad to try to help you with these chores by eating the mop, broom, or papers as you are trying to get the job done. This kind of help does not speed up the process. Pups need to be fed and cared for like babies, in the morning when you are late, and at night when you are tired.

One of our breeders said, "The amazing thing about it is that when a mother sheep has baby sheep, the mother sheep takes care of them. When a mother horse has a baby horse, the mother horse takes care of it. But when a bitch whelps, YOU take care of them!" One puppy is fun, two are a chore, and four or more can be overwhelming if you are not set up for them, and if you do not have the time to devote to them. Eight can be a disaster. Breeders do this as a hobby. It interests them, they have invested time and money — just as you would with any hobby that interests you — in finding the best way to raise pups. Every one of them has early disaster stories to tell.

Finally, what will you do with the pups if you cannot sell them? Eight puppies is a lot of puppies to sell. How long will you keep them? Will you take the responsibility of raising them until suitable homes can be found, or will you simply unload the remainder of the litter on the already overloaded animal shelters? Does your neighborhood have ordinances about the number of dogs you can keep, and how many puppies you can sell before you will be considered a business? What local laws are there in your area concerning your responsibility as the seller? Some states have passed a wide variety of laws within the last several years designed to discourage dog breeding and help eliminate the overflow of unwanted pets. Be sure to check into them before you breed.

If you truly are interested in breeding dogs, go to some shows, talk to breeders, do your homework for the next phase of your hobby just as we have advised throughout this book. Decide what style of dog you want to breed, what temperament you feel a Rottweiler should have, and what purpose you want your puppies to fill in their new homes. Consider that you will need to keep several pups from your first litters in order to see how well your breeding program is working. Do you have room for several Rottweiler adults? Do you have facilities to keep the dogs safe and confined away from each other if they do not get along?

Then, study the pedigrees to find out what bloodlines are most likely to produce the type of dog you want. Decide how you will determine if you are reaching your goal. Will you show them to check their conformation quality? Will you temperament test them, check on the pups after they have been placed in homes, use them as therapy dogs? Will you train them as working dogs? What kind of homes will they fit into, and how will you sell them? What kind of guarantee will you offer new owners?

From a practical standpoint, how will you handle the litter? Look at facilities of other breeders. Ask what kinds of equipment you will need. Ask about vaccinations and eye care. Find a good vet who is familiar with the breed and willing to work with you. Do you have a vet who knows anything about whelping and caring for a litter? Where will you get help if something goes wrong? Do you have the time to socialize them, and a clear idea of how you will do it?

We strongly advise finding a breeder who is willing to work with you as a mentor. They have the experience you will need to tap into and can give you advice along the way if things don't go as planned.

After you have thought out the project completely, do your first breeding. Like anything else, careful planning and forethought can save stress, money, grief and your home!

Some of our breeders recounted how they got started. For many, it was a matter of seeing a dog they liked, investigating his lines and finding the right person to help and advise them. Then they invested as much money as they could afford in the best bitch they could find. Sometimes this worked, but many of our breeders reported starting again and again until they got the right foundation stock, clear of problems and representing the ideal they had in mind for the breed.

There is a lot more to breeding than owning a pet. If you intend to do it, be sure that you do it as well as you can. This will provide you with the best possible chance of producing quality puppies and happy new owners. If this is not the way you intend to pursue breeding, DON'T DO IT. Save yourself time, money, stress and save the animal shelter system the burden of taking on yet another unwanted, improperly cared for litter!

SHOPPING
ARCADE

THE FOLLOWING SECTION IS A SHOWCASE OF FINE COMPANIES WHO PRODUCE AND SELL PRODUCTS WHICH ARE OF INTEREST TO ROTTWEILER OWNERS.

Many of these goods and services you will not find in the course of your normal shopping patterns. Those who are involved with dogs and dog shows are used to finding an abundance of these kinds of products at the many show vendors they see each weekend, but we know that many of our readers do not have the same opportunities. We hope that by presenting these companies to you here, it will make your life with your Rottweiler a little richer and easier. Please feel free to write us and let us know how you feel about this section, or this book in general. We encourage your comments and would like to hear from you. If at any time after publication you cannot make contact with a company listed in this section, or a breeder listed in the breeder sections, please contact Dace Publishing to get an updated number.

ANIMAL ART CONTEST

Any Media - Any breed of dog or type of pet.

*Cash Prizes   *Gift Certificates   *Publication

Division I - Adults   Division II - Jr. - under 20 yrs.

Bi-annual contest - Prizes awarded in each contest!

**NO LIMIT TO THE NUMBER OF ENTRIES,
OR THE NUMBER OF SUCCESSIVE CONTESTS.**

ENTRY DEADLINES: March 30 and Sept. 30

Entry FEE: $15.00 per entry,   *Entry fee must accompany entry.*

Send: Artwork ; name, address and phone number with entry fee.   State age if under 20

Mail to: Dace, P.O. Box 91, Ruckersville VA 22968

PHOTO CONTEST

Categories:

a) humorous   b) action
c) with children   d) dog in landscape
e) puppies   f) general

Do you have some wonderful shots of your Pet? Any breed of dog or type of pet is eligible.

* Cash Prizes
* Gift Certificates
* Publication

Bi-annual contest.— Prizes awarded in each contest!

NO LIMIT TO THE NUMBER OF TIMES YOU CAN ENTER EACH CONTEST OR SUCCESSIVE CONTESTS.

ENTRY DEADLINES: June 30 and Dec 30
All entries received after those dates will be entered in the next contest!

Entry Fee: $15.00 per entry

Send photo with name and address on back, plus name address and phone number with entry fee to:
Dace Publishing,
P.O. Box 91
Ruckersville, VA   22968

Outstanding
Photo

This photo was selected as the outstanding photo submitted by our breeders. It is typical of the original use of the breed. It was submitted by Anne Yatteau who has done some fantastic photos of the breed.

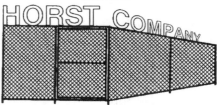

D_{ACE}
Publishing

P.O.Box 91
Ruckersville, VA 22968
(804) 985-3603

Dace Publishing is proud to present the *Basic Guide Breed Series.*
With emphasis on the unique qualities of each breed, we present up to date information on style, health, temperament and suitability of each breed by interviewing breeders across the country. Our titles include:

Basic Guide to the Labrador Retriever   *Basic Guide to the Chinese Shar-Pei*
Basic Guide to the Rottweiler   *Basic Guide to the American Cocker Spaniel*
Basic Guide to the Doberman Pinscher   *Basic Guide to the Great Dane*
Basic Guide to the Dalmation   *Basic Guide to the German Shepherd*
Basic Guide to the Poodle   *Basic Guide to the Dachshund*

With **new titles currently under production.** Order directly, or **call for additional titles** which are being added all the time.
TO ORDER:

Title(s) X $9.95 each, plus **$3.00 shipping and handling for up to five books,** **$.35 for each additional book (Continental U.S.) VA res. add 4.5% sales tax.**

Send name, address, phone number along with payment.
Payment by check, VISA, MC. Include name on card, number and ex. date.
OR CALL FOR DIRECT ORDERING — Orders Only 1-888-840-DACE (3223)

DREAMIN' DOG

BANNER

FLAGS

These Top Quality Flags or Banners of U.S. made, fade resistant nylon in almost any color background. Full size. Banner hangs down with pole sleeve, Flag has grommets.

0601   Banner....$68.00 ea
0602   Flag ...$68.00 ea.
       Specify background color

NATURAL, HOMEMADE
LIVER SNACKS

Avoid snacks made of cereal and other fillers. Your Rottweiler deserves and responds best to a dog's favorite food. These Liver based snacks are a delight to dogs and have been the secret of show, field and obedience kennels for years. Now available for the first time to owners who love their pets and want the best for them.

**Convenient, easy training
treats dogs love!**

0701   Trial size, 6 oz....$3.50
0702   Regular size, 1 lb.......$7.95
0703   Economy size, Full 2 1/4 lbs!......$15.95

TO ORDER: Prices good through 6/97. After which call for availability and current pricing. Include full name and address, item number, quantity, design and/or color where necessary. If using VISA/MC, include number, cardholder name, and expiration date.

DREAMIN' DOG
P.O. 7787
Charlottesville, VA 22906
(888) 840-3223
VA res. add 4.5% sales tax

<u>Shipping/handling:</u>
Orders up to $15.00 add $3.75,
$15. - $50.00 add $4.75,
$50. - $100.00 add $5.75,
$100.- $200.00 add $6.75,
over $200.00 add $9.75

Kriznik Rottweilers